*Success &*

# Change Your Environment Through Your Thoughts

*Success & Happiness Now:*

# Change Your Environment Through Your Thoughts

**Bing Wilson**

To order additional copies of this title, contact your favorite local
bookstore, or visit www.tbmbooks.com

Book design by Melissa Mykal Batalin

The Troy Book Makers, Troy, NY
www.thetroybookmakers.com

ISBN: 978-1-933994-73-4

For more information or to contact the author,
visit www.successwithbing.com

This book is dedicated to all my readers. I want to spark hope in your heart. May this book be a switch that opens your horizon to endless possibilities. May today mark the beginning of a new way of thinking and a new way of living. May your moments be fresh as you learn to savor the present.

# *Acknowledgements*

This is a dream come true for me. I have poured my heart and soul into the pages of this book to touch the hearts of those who wants to create a positive change in their lives.

I could never have done it without the love and support of my husband Kevin. Thank you for your patience and understanding. Thanks to my mother Luz, for teaching me to see beyond the chaos of my young life and injecting me with great work ethic. Thank you for helping me build confidence and courage even in the midst of very trying times in our lives. Thanks to Hank and Sandy, the best father-in-law and mother-in-law anyone can have. Thanks to Michael, my precious son. You make my life a garden of possibilities; you inspire me beyond words can say. Thanks to my wonderful stepchildren, Kaitlyn and Kevin. Thank you for believing in me. Thanks to my brother Sunny, his wife Aissa, and my sister Susan. Cousin Margot and best friends Lisa, Zamina, Dora, thank you for your presence in my life.

My heartfelt gratitude to Melissa Mykal Batalin - Art Director and Manager of Troy Book Makers and Miriam Axel Lute, my editor. Thank you for your excellent work. Thank you for helping me make my dream a reality.

# Contents

## Part 3: Creating a Good Foundation

## Part 4: Attitudes for Success

# Why Do We Need Success and Happiness Now?

There is only one reality, the moment that we occupy each time that we experience each breath of life. Each breath awakens a person to a fresh beginning. Success and happiness must be experienced in each and every moment of your life to make it a part of your true reality. The only true reality is what you create in your mind now. There is a thin layer of border separating what we perceive in our mind and what we actually experience as reality.

I have searched for and studied many happy and successful people over the years, looking for how they have reached their goals. Is it luck? Is it education? Is it effort? Or is it the quality of the present thoughts that are in their minds?

Success and happiness is a unique experience for each individual. One's perception of what success is will influence one's level of satisfaction. Are you searching for fulfillment in your life? Tap into the power of the mind to affect the environment through your thoughts. Your thoughts can shape your life spiritually, physically, and financially.

If you want to be successful and find happiness in your life now, this book will help you understand how to create a life of abundance using the power of your thoughts and how to recreate your environment using your imagination.

Use your mind to direct your actions toward the path of your choice. Your thoughts can change your environment.

# PART I

# Introduction to the Power of the Mind

# CHAPTER I

## Change Your Environment Through Your Thoughts

No problem can withstand the assault of
sustained thinking.

—*Voltaire*

Your thought process is crucial to changing your present
moment into your desired future. Cultivate creative
optimism with true purpose. Being aware of your ability to
change your environment will help you to become vigilant
with your thought process. Guard your thoughts from fears
and doubts. Have full conviction that you will get what
you want. A beautiful future will arrive sooner if you truly
believe. Do not waste your time with doubtful thoughts that
can only pull you away from what you want in your heart.

Value your ability to control your own thoughts. You are
the master of your most precious possession. Your thoughts
can mold the kind of life that you want for yourself.

Change your environment by changing your mental
process. Thoughts have the ability to transform into tangible
reality. How you think completely manipulates the life that
you are now living in. Positive thoughts can give you a
consistently progressing life. Be aware of what thoughts you

entertain in your mind. Dissect good useful information and discard the negative pieces after learning from them. Grasp the positive, helpful information as you learn how you can apply it to your benefit.

Nothing in life is permanent; change is your constant companion. If you want to succeed, make peace with change. Change is needed in order to experience movement. Taking forward steps toward success means actual physical action. If you are afraid of change, you tend to be frozen in time. Refusal to take action or welcome change will get you stuck far behind everyone else. Realize that growth cannot be achieved without change. If you are open to new ideas, you can change the old with the new or simply add new information to enhance what you already knew. Openness welcomes new possibilities to explore for progress. Progress can only be acquired after a positive change. Advancement can only take place after sufficient growth.

If you are a serious student of success, change your mental process to be totally in line with your goals in life. Use positive thoughts to dominate your mind from the moment that you get up in the morning until the time that you go to bed. Have total control of your thought process. You have the freedom to choose what you want to think about regardless of what situation you are in.

Learn to sit back and analyze the likely outcome of any decision you are about to make. Weigh your options. Which one makes the best sense? Your thoughts can be compared to a workshop of an artist. Sculpture your future. Mold the ideal life within your mind. You are an artist constantly recreating your environment to satisfy your needs and desire. There is no limit to your creativity. You can have the life that you want. All you have to do is be aware of your ability to make it happen through your thoughts. Your thoughts can create the picture. Senses within the body react to that beautiful creation, bringing the vision closer to reality.

Your present life is a reflection of what you have indulged in your artistic mind. Now that you know that you are the responsible artist who created your present life, choose a picture of your desired success. Create a reality that you want now. Change your thoughts that you may change your life to that which you desire. Look within yourself to find unlimited potential to become what you want to be. Build a life that you want by using total control of your mind. Make your mind a perfect place to create the future that you want. Your future depends on the thoughts that you have in your mind NOW, at this moment.

Recognize that there are thoughts that can inspire you and empower you. Positive thoughts are like logs you burn to keep the fire of motivation at supreme intensity. Your life is the invention of your very own thoughts. Be careful of your inventions. Create a vision of a great future. Hold that supreme vision in your mind NOW. The only way to acquire that beautiful future is to live it in your head first at this very moment. Once you concretize that vision into your subconscious mind, no one can stop you from achieving it. Imprinted belief within you will drive you to succeed.

There are thoughts that can bring you down. Limiting thoughts can drain you mentally, physically, and financially.

Negative thoughts can eventually drain your bank account. They can make you lose other material possessions that you have accumulated as well. Inability to totally control your own thoughts can make you lose control in many more aspects in your life. Learn to steer clear from these thoughts. Negative thoughts can only wear you out. Without energy, your creative development is put on hold. Negative visualization brings you exactly the same negative outcome in your life.

Your awareness can make a difference to create the life that you want. Know that constant entertainment of negative thoughts, imagining the most terrible life, and complaining about everything that is happening around you will give you exactly the undesirable life that you unconsciously created for yourself. It is therefore very important to go through life with awareness of how thoughts can create the kind of life that is as fun, desirable, and comfortable as you want it to be.

Choose to recognize the information in your head. Are these thoughts enriching or are these thoughts draining? Steer away from draining thoughts. Sometimes you cannot help them. However, when you become aware of it, you have the ability to decide to let it go. Do this exercise over and over throughout the day. You will train your mind to be positive. You can become more creative. Creativity attracts more possibilities. Possibilities allow you to use your knowledge and talent to become productive. Productivity increases your value, giving birth to new successes. You become happier. Life becomes a playground of fun.

Strive to improve your life. The quality of your thoughts

can change your environment. You are never stuck. You are free to live life to the fullest by exercising the power of your mind and faith. Living is also growing. No matter what age you are, there is always a chance for growth. Choose a highly positive thought process to rule your mind so, that you may be able to create the change that you want to make. The confinement of a life of poverty is due to the limitations that a person has allowed himself or herself to believe in. Free your mind from the imprisonment of a life of unhappiness and deprivation. Use your new knowledge of the power of your thought to open the gates to freedom. Mold the life that you want by the quality of your thoughts.

## SUSAN'S STORY

When I was about six years old I found out that I had an older half sister named Susan who lived on another island in the Philippines. My father had dated Susan's mother Lucy in Cebu City while he worked at various odd jobs as a young man. He had a job loading cargo on ships, which he did not like that much. My father was a "mestizo," a term used for Spanish-Filipino. My father had very light skin, which stands out in a country with mostly dark brown skin tones. It is not common to see a "mestizo" working in hard labor jobs, but my father had to take care of himself, since both his parents died at a very young age. My father dreamed of becoming a writer. He eventually landed a job as a news reporter for a newspaper company.

There was an accident that my father was covering, and he met Lucy, who worked as a typist in the police department.

They started dating, and the relationship got serious. Lucy supported him morally and financially because he was a new writer then and did not make that much money. My father taught himself how to write and Lucy supplied him with his writing supplies. Day and night he practiced until he became good at it. When Lucy's family found out about her relationship with my father, however, they disapproved. Then they found out that she was pregnant, her brother and his buddies beat my father up. He was bloody when he escaped. He got into a cargo ship on which his cousin was the captain. He hid in the captain's cabin until the ship reached Davao City.

In Davao, he met my mother. They got married and had my brother and me. Father became a very good writer. He wrote for newspapers and eventually became editor and publisher of the *Mindanao Vanguard*, his very own business. He also became the head of the Department of Public Information in Tagum, Davao del Norte. He was responsible for writing the governor's speeches. I was very proud of him.

When we found out that my father had a child in another city, we were quite surprised in the beginning, but then my whole family went on vacation to Cebu City and met Susan. My brother and I accepted Susan and love her dearly. Years later after the separation of my parents, my mom moved us to the same island where Susan lived. We were able to build a strong bond with my sister.

Susan had her share of hardships, including growing up without a father and being raised by a grandmother who was very strict. When she was a teenager she rebelled. She stopped going to school, eloped with her boyfriend, and secretly got married, to the dismay of her family. There was nothing they could do. Susan bore two beautiful children named Jacky and Rio. However, the marriage did not last. Her husband found work apart from the family and started having affairs. They separated, and Susan took care of her kids alone with no child support from Mario. She struggled for many years, hardly having enough money to buy food for her children.

Years later, Susan came to me and expressed her desire to go back to school. She did not have the money to enroll herself to get back to school, so she asked if I could help her. Without any doubt I knew that my sister was serious and ready to change her environment. Susan knew that without proper education it would be very difficult for her to get out of poverty. She felt that she was physically capable of doing something better with her life. She firmly believed that completing her education would enable her to stand on her two feet and be independent. Her dream was to land a good job as a teacher. My brother Sunny and I supported our dear sister with her education.

Susan became a teacher. She taught for an exclusive school for boys at the University of San Carlos for many years. Life improved a little, but teachers' salaries are low in the Philippines, and it was still a challenge for Susan to support her two kids. She dreamed of coming to America secretly. She found out from a friend about a program to teach in America. She applied for a position in a Culture Exchange Teaching Program, took a very rigorous test, and had an interview. As she waited for the results, she prayed hard and asked her close friends to pray for her. One day, I got a phone call from my sister telling me that she was in Raeford, North Carolina.

I asked Susan, "How did you do it?" Immigration is so strict in the Philippines that it is tough to easily get out of the country. Susan said that she fervently asked God to send her to America. Even through the midst of her difficulties, in her heart and in her mind she knew and felt that there would be a better life for her. She wanted to change her environment so badly that she had no doubt that God would grant her what she wanted. She imagined a better life, with a higher standard of living and being able to send money home to her two teenage daughters. Through her constant prayers, which were like affirmations of belief, Susan's faith became strengthened. Her imagined future became her true reality.

She is currently teaching for the public school system in Raeford. She is very professional with her work. She takes pride in her teaching career, making sure that she gives the children the best learning experience. In North Carolina, she met a retired military man. They fell in love and got married. Susan is contagiously happy now. She is living life to the fullest because she believed that she could, always using her positive thoughts and keeping a great attitude no matter what she was going through.

## CHOOSING YOUR THOUGHTS

Your good thoughts provide positive mental health. The constancy of the same thought can deposit the information into the subconscious mind, making it a part of your belief system. As the belief is embedded within you, it attracts the positive forces of nature to work for you. Faith works in the same manner. The practice of infusing positive thoughts constantly into your mind builds your faith. Nature will grant you what you want if you have fervently asked for it over and over in total faith. Live your life fully with active faith. Action backed up with strong faith can move mountains.

How can you have a spontaneous elimination of negative thoughts and negative energy? At the end of each day, reflect on what went on through the day. If there were things that disappointed you or hurt you, try to learn what you can from them and then let them go completely. Literally imagine the release of negative feelings and thoughts from your heart and mind into the abyss of the universe where they belong. Bury the negativities like useless ashes and kiss them goodbye.

Letting go of ill feelings and draining thoughts will save you more space and time for creative thinking. You will have a clear mind. You will free yourself of unnecessary nuisance. Release all ill feelings and negative thoughts before going to bed. Imagine yourself free from them. You will notice how much better you will feel. You will go to bed in peace, thereby allowing your subconscious mind to work overnight constructively. It is important to think of what you want, imagining the outcome that you desire before going to bed. Condition your subconscious mind to work for you as you sleep, finding ways for you to get to what you truly want in your heart.

Are you like one of the many people who live their lives carrying past burdens, piling new ones on top of the old ones each day? It is like walking the journey of life with huge bricks piled up on the shoulder. Life becomes a timid, undesirable task. Do not fall into this trap of burdensome living. Free yourself. Let go of past heartaches, let go of anger. Forgive people who may have hurt you in the past. Ask anyone whom you think you have offended in the past for forgiveness. Call them. Write them. It can free your soul.

> Forgiveness does not change the past, but it
> does enlarge the future.
> —*Paul Boese*

As you set your soul free, you open up more space for creative thinking. Your creative thinking can bring forth desired changes in your environment. The decision is in your hands.

How Can Thoughts Change Your Environment?
- Through creative optimism
- Through recognition of freedom of choice
- Through letting go of negativity

## How to Conquer Life

The greatest discovery of my generation
is that a human being can alter his life by
altering his attitudes.

—*William James*

Conquer yourself in order to conquer life. There is only one thing that you have total control of, and that is your very own thoughts. Total control of your thoughts makes you the prime driver of your destiny. What dwells within your mind influences your attitude as well as your decisions. Filtering the information that you allow to dominate your mind is vital to paving the path to your success.

I think of my mind as a projector of what my future holds. My thoughts can either make me or break me. There have been times when I have subjected myself to much negativity, with thoughts like, "I need to lose weight . . . If I could only be a few inches taller . . . Why did I not write a book sooner?" The list can keep going on and on, and what happens next is a sadness that sinks within. Now I refuse to navigate my thoughts into a negative discourse. I replace my doubts with positive reinforcement. I do a positive self-talk that uplifts me. I say phrases like, "I look good, I can do it, I deserve it."

Once you let a thought dominate your mind, you have a great chance of soon experiencing that thought in reality. Guard your thoughts against negative impulses. If you allow yourself to be influenced by your own fears, creating alibis along the way, it deteriorates your self-esteem. There are times when other people feed you with negativities: learn to recognize and steer away from these types of influence.

Instead, take total ownership of the most important possession of the human species. The health of your mind is the key that will unlock the door to as much happiness and success you want to have. There is no limit to how much you can have. We live in a free country that encourages those who desire to excel and gives them free rein to get what they work hard for.

On the other hand, inability to control your own mind will make you unable to control anything else in your environment. Thoughts are like materials used in manufacturing the kind of world that you want to experience. Higher quality thoughts create a higher quality of life. Negative thoughts create a negative environment that you will have to endure. This book will awaken your awareness to transform your life. Read this book over and over until you understand the true power of your mind.

> Powerful and mighty is the human mind! It
> builds or it destroys.
> —*Napoleon Hill,*
> author of *Think and Grow Rich*

## SUCCESS AND HAPPINESS ARE STATES OF MIND

Conquer life by being aware of your ability to control what you allow into your thoughts. Protect yourself from negative influences, whether they are ones you imagine or ones suggested by others. Flush your negative imaginary creations. They are useless to you, hindering you from achieving your best. Trust your own willpower to resist negative influence from other people. Distance yourself from people who rob you of your self-confidence. Surround yourself with people who are positive and success-driven. Their influence is what you need to get to where you want to be.

## HOW YOU PERCEIVE LIFE INFLUENCES YOUR ATTITUDE

It is not what the world can give you, but what you can give the world to make it a better place for you. It is in your power to experience a life of utmost abundance by the way you perceive the world. Make your eyes a window out of which there is an awesome view; see life and be in awe of its beauty each moment.

How you see life affects the way you respond to people and circumstances. Choose to see the brighter side of anything you experience. If it becomes a challenge to see something from a positive angle, choose to tame your reaction. A positive attitude is vital for success. Character is exquisitely molded by the attitude you choose to conduct yourself with. A person can have good looks and elaborate education, but if he or she has a bad attitude, the total package is ruined. He or she may as well be walking in the nude, surrounded only by social ignorance. A person with average looks who has great attitude is an enchanting package. A handsome person possessing a great attitude is the ultimate package.

## FIND SOMETHING GOOD IN EVERYONE

Like in an abstract painting, there is hidden beauty in the midst of imperfection. It is not easy for the eye to see what is beneath the surface. The naked eye, if untrained, can only find confusion and chaos when looking at an abstract painting. Train your eyes to search beyond the top and find the good hidden within each human being. Like pieces of art, each human being is unique, and the difference among all people is what makes life interesting. Never judge a person just because of an imperfection or a fault that you see. All human beings are basically good, having the capacity to love and receive love.

Once you are able to see the good in each person you encounter, your experiences with people become more enriching and fun. Immerse yourself in utmost love for humanity. Treat everyone the way you would treat your own family. Pureness of affection and compassion creates a positive energy in your life. We are all connected as a part of the entire creation. Spread the beautiful emotion of love in each of your moments with all the people you encounter. You will increase your happiness and the happiness of the people around you. A heartfelt greeting to a fellow worker or a stranger can be a good start. Allow yourself to discover something good in each human being, and be grateful for their presence. Small gestures of love and thoughtfulness throughout the day can enrich your happiness and the happiness of those around you.

## LOVE AND PEACE CAN GIVE YOU CLARITY

As your heart becomes a natural haven for happiness, you will find yourself immersed in utmost love for life. It will feel good to be alive. Every bone in your body, every cell that composes your human structure will feel awake, full of the energy of life. The awareness that the pure energy of life resides within you can give you peace, because you know your inner core is a foundation of positive, uninhibited pure energy that you can tap into anytime you want to. When you are at peace, your mind functions with clarity. Clarity of mental function enables you to see your goals clearly, which in turn enables you to make sensible decisions. Those decisions affect the quality of your life and the quality of your relationships. A calm, peaceful, well-focused mind is a breeding ground for successful, life-enhancing decisions. Each decision you make affects your situation for better or for worse. To turn it for the better, each decision and action needs to be in line with the values you hold in your heart.

Making decisions and acting upon things with the sole purpose of satisfying yourself can actually turn your situation for the worse. In the end, a selfish life lived only for one's personal satisfaction becomes a very lonely way to exist. You can become a lone man on an island. Selfishness equals loneliness. Who in their right mind wants to be unhappy? It is a human need to be happy, to feel good, to feel connected, to feel accepted.

## SECRET TO TRUE HAPPINESS IS PEACE

Conquer life with your awareness that you have the secret to true happiness. That secret is finding peace within the core of your being. Knowing that you have the power to create a life that you want. Use your decision to make a big difference in your happiness. The seed sits within the soul. Serene peace increases your patience with the changes and challenges of life. Patience gives room for flexibility, allowing you to glide through tough times. Patience gives you time to think and be more rational, gaining power over your emotions.

## GIVING LOVE CAN GIVE YOU BLISS

Conquer life with love. It all starts with love. Love makes you gain happiness, peace, and patience. Love can conquer all unhappiness. Overall love can enhance your attitude toward life itself. Attitude is vital to your success. Your success and happiness does not depend on what is happening around you and how others treat you. Your happiness and success depends upon your consistent positive attitude toward people, situations, and life itself. Experience bliss in each moment as love emanates from within you, creating a strong foundation for success and happiness.

To Conquer Life You Need to Have:
Clear Vision
Love
Positive Attitude

Write down 10 steps you can take to conquer life each day:

1. _____
   _____

2. _____
   _____

3. _____
   _____

4. _____
   _____

5. _____
   _____

6. _____
   _____

7. _____
   _____

8. _____
   _____

9. _____
   _____

10. _____
    _____

# CHAPTER 3

## *Your Future Depends on the Decisions You Make Today*

Self-discipline is the strength of will to do what is right. This power of will is derived from a thinking mind combined with a passion for positive action. The mind rules the decisions that you make in every situation. Give yourself room to weigh things in proper perspective so that each decision you make is in line with your enlightened values, morals, and principles.

Life is composed of a sequence of decisions. I remember as a child, my mother instilled in us the importance of education. She said that education is important to have a better future. As young as I was, I made a definite decision to graduate from college. I wanted the education badly, knowing that it could elevate our standard of living. I also wanted my mother to be proud of me. It was difficult, however, to see how I would accomplish this goal because we were poor. Still, I remember knowing within myself that I could and I would, no matter what. The conviction inside was strong and fervent.

Once I believed that I could do it and made the decision to go for what I wanted to accomplish, the rest followed, an unfolding of the future that I had foreseen. Growing up in the Philippines, life was a constant struggle. The decisions I made allowed me to get out of the tough cycle. I graduated from college at age 20.

Then I had to make a decision whether to seek employment or to keep expanding the small dressmaking business I had started in the basement where we lived. I went to see a few of my former classmates who were employed at TV stations and other business offices to see if they were enjoying their work. They seemed to be happy with the work that they did, just as happy as I was running my business. What I loved most about owning a business, however, was the freedom to do what I want to do with my time. I owned the business, so I got to run the show. Also, the harder I worked the more I made. So I decided to keep on working for myself.

I approached Lola Lillian Borromeo, the owner of a newly built store space near my home. She owned many buildings along the busy road where I lived at that time, including the basement my family occupied. Lola Lillian had known my family for many years. She used to have clothes altered by my mother. She was a very kind hearted lady. After seeing the condition of our former dwelling, she had invited my family to live for free in the basement of one of her many buildings. So, as I saw a store space being built attached to other buildings owned by the Borromeos, I knew I had to make a move quickly or someone else would take the great spot. I told my mother about the plan; she told me to go for it. I immediately went to Lola Lillian's residence, bringing gifts with me. I gave her a dress that I had made and a basket of fruit. I told her that I was interested in renting the store space as soon as it became available. Aware of the fact that she might be skeptical about renting a space to someone so young, let alone someone who lived in her basement apartment rent free, I convinced her to give me a chance for three months to see if my business would thrive. If not, I promised I would vacate the premises immediately. I also offered to start paying for the basement apartment we were living in at the time.

Business went very well and I was never late with my rent for the five years that I used that business space. It's important to make decisions if you want to go down a new path. Do not hesitate to make that very important decision that can change your life.

Decisions are life-changing events. Each one steers you in a direction of your choice. Each thoroughly thought-out choice brings about some changes that can possibly improve your life. Take all your decisions seriously, because what you decide can have a direct effect on the kind of life that you live. Inability to make decisions can make you a victim of circumstance. It is easy to fall into passive existence, swaying through life, aimlessly living with whatever comes your way. Then one day you wonder, "Why am I in this situation? Why do I not have enough money to survive? Why do I suffer from so many illnesses? Why is my family falling apart? Why did I lose my job? What did I do to deserve this? Where did I go wrong? How can I make it better? Is there a way out of this?"

Yes indeed, there is a way out from the passive existence in which a person sometimes becomes entrapped. Discover your freedom; start using your will to truly exist by participating in creating your own destiny. Decide to use your mind as a ground to cultivate positive thoughts that can enhance each decision that you make. You have the power to translate your positive thoughts into driven desire that can escalate into well-planned actions for the betterment of the environment that you live in. You are free to create the kind of life that you want using decisions that can help you to acquire your central goal in life. A well-focused mind with a central motivation to succeed creates decisions that elevate your quality of life. A mind without a strong focus will not use its full potential.

Do you want to participate in choosing the direction your life takes you, or would you rather just sit and relax and be driven by the waves of time? Make up your mind. The difference between someone who likes to drive and someone who wants to be driven is a matter of their state of mind. If you are seeking success and happiness, take the driver's seat and decide to take charge of your life. Be the person who decides which road to take and which turn to make. Take responsibility for each decision and each action within your lifetime so that you will not regret what could have been or should have been. A person who likes to take the back seat can fall asleep and end up somewhere other than where he or she truly wanted to be.

Do not cry for the past. Live in total consciousness of the present to create a better tomorrow. Your future depends on the decisions and choices you make today and hereafter. Each decision is a turning point that transforms your situation. Success is achieved through countless decisions that pave the way toward that brighter tomorrow. What you do now is what is important. Decisions that you make guide your actions.

They can be life changing, life enhancing, and sometimes the key to a dramatic elevation of your status in life.

When you need to make a decision, do you change your mind often? Do you find it difficult to make a decision and stick with it long enough to see how effectively it can work for you? Do you change your mind so fast that you are unable to see the results of your first decision?

Not all decisions are effective, but each is an important step in the learning process. The discipline not to give up when things are most trying can ultimately bring you your desired success.

Inability to make a decision can also hurt your situation. Make a decision quickly after a good assessment of the facts involved in the situation. A good leader makes the necessary decision to move forward or to halt: not deciding on what is needed creates uncertainty. It makes a person seem to not know what they are supposed to do. Procrastination in making a decision can make you miss a lot of opportunities. Making up your mind about what to do and doing it as quickly as possible will bring about the kind of change you need to progress. Things will start to happen; movement forward is a good sign that you are getting closer to your goal. Keep an eye on where each decision is taking you. Setbacks may require you to make a new turn.

If, after some time, a decision does not bring about forward movement toward your goals, then it is time to make a new decision. Movement forward is the key for progress. The more steps forward the better.

## DO YOU NEGLECT TO ADDRESS
## YOUR PROBLEMS PROMPTLY?

Do you at times pretend that a problem is not there? Pretending to ignore a problem allows the problem to gain ground and grow. A growing problem usually ends up with disastrous result if not caught and addressed early on. Always address a problem in its infancy. Pretending to be too busy to notice the problem is like driving on a highway with a flat tire: continuing to drive even after knowing that you have a busted tire will ruin the wheel as well, busting it beyond repair. Imagine driving on a highway in an imbalanced vehicle with one tire blown off. If you continue to pretend that nothing is going on, pretty soon you will be driving on the rim of the wheel. The car can catch fire or the imbalance can cause you to lose control of the car and have an accident. This example is extreme, but this is similar to what happens when any problem or trouble is not addressed quickly.

There are certain problems that you do need time to ponder to get to the right solutions. That is different from ignoring them. Use your own discretion, and address the problems that need immediate attention promptly. Meanwhile, use as much time as you need, and all the possible resources you have, to get to an intelligent positive solution to those problems that need serious manipulation to resolve.

It is not that I'm so smart, it's just that I
stay with the problems longer.
*—Albert Einstein*

## DO YOU FEEL STRESSED BY YOUR PROBLEMS?

Has stress gotten to you? Have you experienced being so overwhelmed by stress that you become easily angry and irritable? Stress is a great burden when you allow it to occupy your entire mind. One stressful thought on top of another stressful thought creates a poisonous toxicity that feeds into your whole mental system. What is in your mind affects your character as well as your health. Using your mind as a bank of stressful negative impulses crowds it, making it lose space for clear creative thinking. Under these conditions, you can become easily angry, taking your frustrations out on your loved ones and your associates.

A problem can only become stressful if you perceive it that way. Stress is a human defensive invention. It is an excuse to feel bad, a way to surrender to defeat. Face the situation or problem squarely head on and it will cease to be stressful. Understand the root of the problem. Ask yourself why you feel the way you do. Write down a list of possible ways to resolve the problem. From that list, create an organized plan of how you will fix the problem. Even when fixing the problem will not be completed immediately, at least you know that it can be resolved. Let it go.

Giving up on a problem without taking a chance to resolve it shuts the door to any kind of solution. All you have left is stress in your mind. Stress deteriorates your capacity for creative thinking.

If you are already stressed, try meditation to help you relax. There are a lot of books and audio books that you can borrow from your local library to help you learn meditation techniques and breathing techniques to help you release stress. Invest in your mind: buy books that can help you get in touch with your peaceful deeper self, that quiet spot that you need to visit every now and then to recharge your batteries.

## ARE YOU FINDING SOLACE IN ALCOHOL, DRUGS, OR CIGARETTES?

Excessive use of alcohol, drugs, or cigarettes to escape from reality is like building your own prison cell. Unable to face daily realities, a person who starts using addictive substances gets entrapped in his or her very own habits. Getting hooked can deteriorate the mind and the body. Addiction entails a total loss of freedom when it gets out of hand. An addicted person loses total control. If one cannot control oneself, how can one control anything else in life?

My father, for example, was a very gifted writer. His downfall was his battle with his drinking problem. As far back as I can remember my father drank a lot. He drank whatever was available: liquor, beer, or wine. If he was not drinking, he was constantly nursing a cup of coffee and a cigarette. He could be a most loving, caring, and generous person when not under the power of alcohol. I remember him telling me huge dreams that he had. He would say, "One day I will start my own fertilizer business. I will make a lot of money." My mother told me that my father had also dreamed of owning a bookstore, since he loved to read.

But once he started to drink again, he simply could not stop. His character deteriorated as the alcohol took total control of his system. He became very argumentative. He would argue with people that he was drinking with, including strangers, and he picked fights with my mom when he got home. It was traumatic for us. My brother and I cried a lot when the fights went on. There were other times when my dad got so drunk that we would all lock ourselves in one room, bringing with us the pot of rice and some other food to sustain us until he sobered up. Alcoholism was great burden for us, as it is for many families.

Take total responsibility for your life. Uphold your self-worth by exercising your willpower to say no to the temporary relief of addictive substances. The mind rules your behavior, decides what is best for you. Success can only be attained when you are able to have total control of your mind. Health is achieved by intelligent choices, so use a strong will to stay away from addictive substances that can destroy your health.

Moderate use of alcohol is good especially when drinking wine with dinner or when socializing. Red wine is good for the heart. A glass or two once a week is healthy. But drinking excessively to drown your sorrows or to find excitement until you lose control of yourself can be dangerous to your health. Using alcohol as a stress reliever, however, can lead to addiction, which creates a new problem with greater consequences. Your judgment can become impaired and you can lose sight of what is truly good for you. Your family suffers and your productivity at work declines. If you are serious about succeeding, take control of your habits. Steer clear of devastating habits that can eventually become addictive and imprison you and your senses in a world that can only go spiraling down to failure. If you cannot control your drinking, then quit it before it ruins your life and your family.

## ARE YOU MAKING A BIG DEAL
## OUT OF SMALL MATTERS?

Prevent exaggerating problems for the sense of extra drama. Making a big deal out of small things can aggravate your family, friends, and associates. You do not need attention drawn to you for petty things. Try to find quick solutions to simple problems. It is not worth spending time feeling bad for small matters; let it go. If you do not, people will not take you seriously the next time you talk about a problem, even if the new problem might truly warrant serious attention. All people will remember are the numerous times you have overly inflated your problems.

Take the less emotional route to address issues that are minuscule. Learn to tolerate small petty situations and not be annoyed by small maters. Tolerance is the key to keep your peace throughout the day. Annoyance can take your focus away from all the more important matters that need to be addressed.

## ARE YOU AFRAID TO ASK FOR HELP?

Are you too shy or too afraid to ask for help? Do you feel inadequate when you ask for assistance? Are you afraid of rejection?

Let me share with you what I learned when I attended the one week Breakthrough to Success Seminar with Jack Canfield. In one exercise, we were taught to ask for what we want. They paired us with people to practice. We learned to ask for the most difficult, outrageous things. We had a good time laughing at some of the questions asked. For example: "Can you lend me your house for a week?" "Can you pay for my mortgage?" "Can you buy me a car?" After a lot of practice, we were given the exercise to ask someone, whether a family member or a stranger, for something that was a stretch. The next day we shared the type of answers we got. What was truly amazing was how the exercise eased our individual inhibitions. The more you are able to ask for what you want, the more doors will open up for you.

If you struggle with these problems, ask yourself what you have to lose. The worst thing that can happen is for someone to say no to you. You will never find out what chances you have until you ask. Many opportunities are lost only because of someone's inability to ask the question. Practice asking questions facing the mirror. Ask your reflection the most unusual request you can think of. Do this exercise every day until you increase your confidence, preferably in the morning while getting ready to go into the shower, so you are also setting a tone for your day. During the day while at work or while interacting with friends practice asking questions that are a bit of a stretch for you. Keep doing this for a few weeks, and you will be tremendously surprised how people will react. There are a lot of people willing to share what they know, a lot of people willing to help another human being. All you have to do is have the courage to ask.

It is good to be resourceful: the more help you get, the more information you acquire, the more you can accomplish.

Recognize the skills and expertise of others. When more minds are involved, you are able to gather more information. Pulling these resources together to arrive a particularly important goal can be very powerful. Consult many experts, gather a good amount of information, and analyze all the facts before making a major decision.

Be tenacious in deciphering the information you get, but then make quick decisions. Inability to make a quick decision after getting all the details can cause a lot of money lost and opportunities lost. While you delay, other go-getters will get ahead of you owning what supposedly could have been yours, if only you had made up your mind fast enough.

A person who wants to succeed must learn to overcome the fear of asking for what he or she needs and wants. Sometimes you can get what you need and want just by throwing the question out there and observing what happens. Asking a question can open a lot of doors of opportunity for you.

## PERSEVERE TO SUCCEED

It is not enough to just dream. Discipline your mind to get up each morning with purpose. Imagine how your day will unfold smoothly. Think things through as you plan the steps you have to take to make your dreams come true. What it takes is a strong, disciplined mind that perseveres through time. The mind develops strength. Overcoming trials becomes an exercise. On the other hand, each failure is a lesson that invigorates the success-driven, disciplined individual to strive harder to climb up from the fall. Do not relax in the pit after a fall. Staying in the dark pit for too long will not be good for your ego. Being stuck in a bad situation for too long destroys your self-esteem. Gather what is left of your energy to find the courage to climb. Find your way out so that you may continuously move up a step at a time, a decision at a time. Each disciplined step brings you closer to your desired future.

Decisions that you make today are vital for your success. Success is not dependent on luck. Luck is what you create for yourself. Awareness of your very own capacity to create your luck will launch you on your true search for a better tomorrow. Use total control of your mind with complete discipline of your thought process, allowing only the positive thoughts to dominate your mind throughout the day, filtering out negative thoughts and immediately dismissing them. Replace negativities with positive, progressive thoughts for more luck.

You are reading this book because you are searching for something better. You want to find success and happiness NOW. Learning the messages within this book about the use of the mind will give you the key to finding your luck. You are responsible for your own luck and your own future: the key is in your hand.

Good Decisions Are Made Through:
Discipline
Courage

# CHAPTER 4

# Reject Negativities to Make Space for Growth

There is nothing so useless as doing efficiently
that which should not be done at all.

*—Peter Drucker*

Do you want to be successful? Why not? You just need to find the way to where you truly want to be. Each of us wants to achieve success whether we admit it or not. The first step in opening the road to success is getting rid of negativities, most especially the ones that you entertain in your mind. Doubts, fears, insecurities, and ill thoughts about others can hinder you from starting your journey, a challenge that needs to be overcome.

What are the conversations you have with yourself? Do you say, "I am too fat, I am too short, I am too afraid to try something new, I am so afraid to change my ways"? Change the negative self-talk to, "I will start eating healthy, I feel good about myself, I welcome change because change can help me improve my situation for the better."

I remember as a child, drawing buildings and houses on pieces of paper. As I drew those pictures, I recall saying to myself that one day I will own many houses and many buildings. I was only seven years old, but I had big dreams. Now I am an adult and own many rental properties with my husband. We have several projects going on at the same time. We are developing land for commercial purposes and condominiums. The conversations you have in your mind with yourself can affect the actual life that you will experience.

When I was six years old and finishing kindergarten, there was a graduation ceremony held for the graduating students. We wore white little robes with white caps. The names of the students were called one at a time and each one came to the stage to get a certificate. The certificate was handed over, hands were shaken. The student stayed on the stage near a microphone. My brother, who was about nine years old, was assigned to ask this question to each little graduate: "What do you want to be when you grow up?"

One child said, "When I grow up I want to be a doctor." Another said, "When I grow up I want to be a lawyer." On and on, the dreams of each student were announced on the microphone while the parents stood so proud, frantically taking pictures and clapping their hands. When my brother asked me what I wanted to be when I grew up, I said: "When I grow up I want to be a flight stewardess." In my mind, I imagined wearing the beautiful uniforms, shoes, and hats just like the ones in the magazines. I admired the beautiful, sharp-looking ladies pictured in those magazines. I thought that it would be such a fun thing to do to fly all over the world.

As I grew up, though, my dream seemed to die. I did not grow tall enough to make the height requirement. They used to have extremely strict height and weight requirements for flight stewardesses. So as I matured I did not dare to entertain that old dream. Many years passed and I was in America. I worked in my first husband's business until I found myself divorced. I got myself a job at a collection law firm in New York City, which I enjoyed tremendously, but three years later business was down and I got laid-off. I decided to pack my bags and moved to San Diego with my young son and my mother. It was a difficult move because I loved New York but it was time for me to go. I had lost my focus after I got laid-off and was enjoying my single life a little too much. I knew that if I wanted to be able to get back on my feet again I needed to do something drastic. For me a change of environment was what I needed. I called up my brother Sunny and told him that I was ready to take him up on his offer to live with his family.

For many years in the Philippines, I was the one that took care of the family's financial needs, but at that point I was the one that needed help. I swallowed my pride and told my brother that I would look for a job aggressively and move out as soon as I got myself back on track. It was a weekend when we arrived in San Diego, but I did not waste time. I asked my brother to help me with my resume, got it typed, and bought the Sunday paper on Saturday evening. I faxed fifty resumes each day for three straight days.

On Monday, I looked through the paper to make sure that I did not miss any job classified ads, and there right in front of me was a large print ad from a major airline for a sales representative. I faxed my resume immediately. A few hours later, I received a phone call asking me if I would be interested to come in for an interview. The person on the other line made it a point to let me know that it only paid seven dollars an hour. Enthusiastically, I told them I didn't mind at all. In my mind, the old dream was coming back to life. All I wanted was to get into the airline industry and move around to other positions later on.

After several interviews with other companies, I accepted the job with a major airline. Within four months, I achieved tier-one status, becoming one of the top sales representatives in the company. Within seven months I put in my application for the flight attendant position. I flew down to Pittsburgh and went through the grueling interview process twice. Each time, I dressed just like a flight attendant: I wore my high heel shoes, chose the best suit I could find, and put my hair up in a nice bun. I applied makeup conservatively. I felt as though I were a flight attendant on those days. I remembered pilots looking my way. I thought to myself, "He must think that I am a flight attendant." I walked with so much confidence. When they told me to get the drug test I was euphoric because I knew that I had gotten the job. I was in seventh heaven, knowing that my childhood dream had finally come through. I wanted to work on those flights.

I remember using the public phone in the Pittsburgh International Airport to tell my family that I believed I was about to get hired. Back in San Diego, days later, I got called to attend the next training session. I jumped up and down as though I had won the lottery. I remembered my brother looking at me with a smile on his face, saying, "Dreams do come true Sis. No matter how long it takes." We both laughed, and the whole family celebrated.

Life has its ups and downs. Whether you are up or down what is important is that you keep cultivating positive self-talk within your mind. These conversations you have with yourself will help in negating your doubts, fears, and insecurities.

## REJECT NEGATIVE INFLUENCE FROM OTHERS

To become successful, you must protect yourself from the negative influence of others. It is a challenging task in the beginning. Some people love controversy. There are people who spend a lot of time talking about others. Some simply cannot stop recounting about many unhappy aspects of their lives. Do not absorb the negative impulses from others. Imagine yourself protected by a light of positive energy repelling the negative forces coming from people around you. When someone speaks ill of another person, do not contribute to the negative conversation. Find a way to change the topic and turn it into something positive. Otherwise, find a good excuse to walk away. Say something like, "Excuse me, I forgot to return a phone call, I have to go" or "Pardon me, I have to get back to work."

### How to Repel Negative Influences

Create a mental state of mind that automatically repels negative influences. Imagine negative influences as rubbish with a foul smell, swarming with worms, and having a strong destructive capacity. Allowing a negative influence into your mind will start a slow decay of the gift of life. When you allow others to negatively influence your thoughts, absorbing this type of energy, it has a disruptive effect on your own physical health. People who are constantly taking in negativities whether from outer influences or within their own minds are those who easily get sick. When the mind is filled with rubbish thoughts, it weakens the body's defenses against infection, making the body more susceptible to diseases. Discouraging influences, when allowed in, can ruin your health as well as take you off track from your goals. To keep yourself healthy, be vigilant about what influences you allow in. Make sure that what you allow in can contribute to your overall health. You have total control of your own mind. No one can make you take in what you despise.

Be constantly conscious of the influences around you. Block the entrance of negative energy by making a choice not to allow it into your precious mind. Shielding your mental state can make you stay focused, with undivided attention on your goals.

## Do the Actions and Language of Other People Bother You?

There are so many things around that can influence how you feel inside. If someone hurt you through spoken words, do you try to hurt them back with your own collection of hurtful words? To hurt someone for the main reason of inflicting pain back toward another person is to stoop into a low-level irrational behavior. Use self-control to make intelligent choices before taking actions.

When someone hurls insulting, painful language toward you, do not take it personally. Think about what is going on inside the mind of the person who loses their composure to make them say these unkind words. Insecurity and fear are probably dominating their mind. Allowing yourself to absorb pain from the giver of the pain is allowing the other person's insecurity to influence you. Use calming words with a low, soothing tone of voice to suppress the anger and pain of the other. A very understanding tone of voice can work magic. Tell the other person that you understand how they feel. Just let them be. Allow them to vent without judging them.

If someone very angry physically pushes you, do you push them right back harder? Defend yourself by all means, but do not consciously intend to cause someone pain .The person who becomes physically aggressive enough to cause someone physical pain has totally lost control. The chaos within their thoughts has exploded into the chaotic environment this person has created for themselves.

What dwells in the mind materializes into the environment. Let your awareness guide you. It is easy to fall into the trap of unconsciously allowing others to negatively influence your inner feelings. You have total control of your own mind. Your mind is your most precious possession, and no one else can tamper with it without your permission.

Along with internalizing outer influences, how you feel inside is affected by your emotions. Remember that your emotions are not attached to you. You can choose to release them and let them go.

In your daily dealings with people, stay aware of whether an incoming influence is negative and disruptive to your emotional state and peace of mind. Make a quick decision to repel and not allow any negative outer influence to dwell within you. Negative, disruptive emotions can break the liquidity of your mental energy flow.

## Is Someone Verbally Abusing You?

Are you in a relationship with someone who is constantly finding fault in you? Is there someone nagging you about different issues all the time? Are you tired of hearing an old broken record playing over and over? If you are a person suffering from constant verbal nagging and abuse, stop and assess your relationship. Ask yourself why this person has not ceased with the verbal garbage.

Think of a way to improve in areas that seem reasonable for change. Then work to improve yourself. Get some counseling together and try to resolve the matter. However, if no matter what you do, this individual finds other things to complain about you, it may be time to find out whether it is even worth being in a relationship with this person at all. Constant nagging and criticism is very damaging to anyone's confidence. You need peace of mind to succeed. Find a supportive partner in life who sees the good in you and encourages you, seeing your strengths instead of your weaknesses.

## Detachment From Other People's Problems

Loved ones, friends, and acquaintances will share their problems with you. Listen to understand, but do not internalize the problem. Constantly worrying about them can consume you. It can make you less productive. To be productive, a mind must be free from worries. Becoming one with the problem can pull you down into the mud of nothingness.

Practicing detachment from other people's troubles enables you to look at the problem from the outside. Clinging to the problem and making it your own, on the other hand, can only crowd your mind, making you unable to think clearly. Free yourself of worries, whether self created or adopted from others. Guard yourself against useless worries. Recognize the obstacle and release it. Releasing worries opens up space for productive thinking, enabling the mind to find ways to create solutions wherever necessary.

If someone drains you with constant complaining about work, family, and life, assess your relationship with this person. Hopefully you have a strong enough energy to convert this person to become more positive. However, if this person is stubborn, it may be a good idea to keep a bit of distance to get some breathing space.

Your success is not dependent on how others treat you. Your success is dependent on your focused commitment on your goals in life. As long as you know in your heart that you have treated others fairly, don't feel bad about how others have treated you. The opinions of others do not make you who you are. Allowing others to affect you is like welcoming negative energy into your system. Negative thoughts and negative energy, whether they are coming from others or are your very own creation can make you feel irritable, angry, and tired. Constantly allowing other people's behavior to bother you will make your daily life feel like a burden. Why make your mind and body a storage facility for toxic energy? Think of yourself as protected by the divine light. You are strong enough to repel negative thoughts and negative energy that can hinder you from achieving happiness and success.

## FRIENDSHIP

Why do we need friends to achieve success and happiness now? No one can survive alone. We all need one another. That secure feeling of being connected to others builds self-confidence within. Confidence generates a better attitude toward life, which can only improve our present reality. To succeed in life we need the feeling of belonging, of building strong relationships as each moment passes, of helping and supporting each other as we go through life. Treat all people with warmth that you may increase the circle of friends that you keep.

The best fun memories of youth are those we share with cherished friends. Growing up is filled with playful times of innocence entwined with joy. Early friendships develop the social skills we need in the adult world. They enable us to learn to trust other human beings. Mutual connection experienced in deep friendship becomes an anchor to the participating souls. You will never feel alone. You are surrounded with people who care for you. All you need to do is call. Friendship can sometimes outlast marriages, though a marriage based on true friendship can be very strong and lasting. It is wonderful to go home to someone you love who understands you as a friend as well, someone with whom you can share all your experiences and dreams, and someone who understands you no matter what.

A true friend is patient with your moods. There will always be a shoulder to lean on when life seems rough. A friend will laugh with you and cry with you. You celebrate each moment of triumph together, glorious with each other's successes. Shared moments increase the bond, solidifying the mutual support. Give to your friend beyond what is expected. There is so much more pleasure in seeing someone enjoy your generosity than there is in receiving. Give of yourself in total abundance.

Mutual loyalty in the friendship bond is strong, like a bridge that connects two islands. Friendships withstand storms and adversities. Cultivate your friendships. Be a loyal and loving friend. Friends have a way of brightening up your day. They ease your burden and help you carry your load in the path of life.

## Who are Your Friends?

Sit back and reflect on what you can learn about yourself from the type of people you spend time associating with. Do your friends add to your state of happiness? Do your friends inspire you? Do they motivate you to do the best in your endeavors? Do you and your friends think alike? When gathered as a group, is the energy positive?

Meeting of the minds can make a group of friends a powerful group. A group of people with common positive outlook can use this as a platform to enrich each other. When two or more people experience a mental merging of great thoughts, a lot of good can take place. Enthusiasm for life increases, ideas start to come alive, and power is gained. United power gained from the positive thoughts of several people becomes a catalyst for greater possibilities. Therefore, it is very important to be involved with a group of people who are seeking similar goals of growth.

People can also use the power of their mind unintentionaily as a negative coalition. A group of people gathered together to discuss miseries, complaints and a dark outlook in life is a good example. Blaming all their miseries on others except themselves. Helplessness will radiate throughout such a group as a mass breakdown of confidence; if anger is the most common topic spoken about in the gathering it will spread into a massive feeling of aggression. Shattered confidence increases hopelessness. Too much anger and aggression can escalate to violence. Negative groups can either compound feelings of defeat or anger, which can be disastrous.

Assess the type of friends you associate with. Choose friends who are highly positive and highly motivated in life. The circle of friends that you consciously choose to associate with can help keep your mind more positive, giving you a great feeling every time you are with them. Friends can make you feel alive, adding healthy years to your life. Humans are social beings; positive influence from others is vital to the quality of life ahead.

### Is a Friend in Love with Misery?

Is there anyone whom you consider to be a friend who seems to be in constant misery? Do you feel that this person is transferring damaging negative influence to you by their negative views? Does this person have a domineering, dark outlook on life? Do you feel that this person is constantly leaning against the door of misery? With hope that you can join him or her as the door swings open? Be aware of the negative influence of this type of person. This person is not a true friend; he or she is a disguised enemy hindering you from becoming a better person by dragging you along the dark path. Being associated with this person can be draining.

Choose your friends. Distance yourself from people who are constantly looking at life in the most negative way. They can only hinder you from getting into the fast lane of growth for success. Surround yourself with people who can influence you for the better. Positive people are your true friends. Together you uplift each other. A true friend is helpful, taking your hand along the lighted path of progressive growth. There is a consistent exchange of positive influence between true friends. The bond is strengthened by the common will to excel in many aspects of life. You assist each other in opening the golden door to success.

### Who Encourages You in Your Endeavors?

Is there someone who gives you a lot of moral support to go the extra mile? How do you feel every time you interact with this person? Do you feel energized to keep working on your goals after being around this person?

A positive family member, friend, or associate who encourages you is a good influence to have around. Cultivate closer relationships with people who are understanding and supportive of your goals. This type of person can help you build your confidence, and he or she will be happy for your success, cheering you to the finish line. In return you can give your support, sharing your great ideas and encouragement. This type of relationship becomes profitable for both parties.

### Who Cautions You Too Much?

A person who is too cautious in life and business can influence you in the same manner. Too much caution can make a person reluctant to take risks. Being close to a person who is constantly too afraid will instill fear in you. Fear can scare you out of doing the next step to accomplish your goals in life. Financial growth happens only after taking many calculated risks. Make sure that you do not adopt and internalize the fears of others. Fear is the root of inaction.

Use rational thinking in weighing things, so that you can see beyond the fear. Make the final decision by how you feel and by what you believe is right. Do not let others make decisions for you. Be the one to take responsibility for the decisions that you make. Success is achieved through the many decisions that steer you to the right path. Take your decisions seriously and make them quickly. Each is a step closer to acquiring your goal in life.

Why You Need True Friendship for Success and Happiness:
Acceptance
Understanding
Loyalty
Support

### Is There Anyone Who Discourages You?

If someone close to you discourages you about the many aspects of your life, you must distance yourself from this individual. Discouraging comments and remarks from someone you associate with can drag you down. How can you get motivated to improve, grow, and achieve success? How can you think clearly when someone is constantly feeding you doubts and fears? How can you make plans when your mind is distracted? How can you make the first action step toward your goal when someone is pulling you away in the opposite direction? How can you unleash that burning desire from within you when someone keeps pouring cold water to kill your fire?

Awareness of getting this type of influence from the people around you is of vital importance so you can shield yourself from it. Tolerate, ignore, and release any discouraging comments and remarks that can hinder you from your goals. Focus on what you want, and have faith that you are capable of acquiring your goal.

### Is There Someone Helpful in Your Life?

Do you have a friend with a big heart? How do you feel around this person? Do you feel grateful for the presence of such a wonderful thoughtful human being? Do you feel that this person adds to your overall well-being? A person with awesome qualities like this deserves love and praise. In return, make sure to help them with anything that they may need. It is a healthy reciprocal process that allows both parties to experience support while growing together in mutual respect.

## LESSEN THE NEGATIVE
## INFLUENCE OF THE MEDIA

Our society is bombarded by negative news from different sources. It seems there is a hunger for sensationalism and drama, and the media feeds this need effectively. Flipping through the television channels during the news hour becomes a very depressing experience, full of pictures of people getting blown away in war, someone getting raped in the next neighborhood, and disasters of different magnitude. It seems that the world is falling apart on all angles. No wonder that our society has become so heavily burdened and people are walking around looking depressed and angry.

Aside from the drama addiction, we are also a society obsessed with celebrities, in awe of their lifestyles and their excessive income. Inadequacy surfaces because we constantly compare ourselves to our idols. We are mesmerized by the daily bombardment of images and information that we take in. We spend so much time in front of the television and the computer that we unconsciously deprive ourselves of the time we need to grow.

Ingesting negative information from the television, newspapers, magazines, and Internet can be depressing. No wonder why so many people in our society are at the mercy of medication that is supposed to make them happier. The effectiveness of such medication, however, is superficial and temporal. Happiness is achieved through your awareness of the power of your choices and decisions. Decide to be happy. Choose to entertain positive material for your senses. It is important to plan ahead. Pick a show that is of quality, an uplifting comedy or something educational. Spend less time with depressing shows so that you may find time for personal growth and precious time with your loved ones.

## WELCOME POSITIVE INFLUENCES

Let your awareness guide you toward positive influences as well as shield you from the negative ones. Filter the kind of influences you allow in from around you, whether the form of the media or other people. Allow only the positive influences to take root in your mind and body. Good thoughts can give you enthusiasm, positive people can inspire you, and positive, educational television programs and reading materials can help you grow. What matters is your ability to control your most valuable possession, your mind. Use your mind as a magnet for success. Do not let anyone tamper it. No one can unless you allow it.

## SUCCESS IS ACHIEVED THROUGH POSITIVE GROWTH

As an individual, you need to provide yourself an atmosphere conducive to learning and acquiring new knowledge to arm you for your journey toward your goal. Feed yourself with helpful, positive information. Learn something new each day. Keep your mind alert to opportunities that present themselves. Make it a habit to read a book each week. Listen to educational audio books while you work out to make your mind and body fit simultaneously. Do not waste precious time while driving your car: listen to audio books while you navigate the world.

Education must be a continuous process. As long as you

live, you must learn new things. It is like savoring a breath of fresh air in the midst of springtime. Learning gives you a feeling of infinite connection to the large pool of universal knowledge. That connection is like a magnetic pull that draws consciousness to what truly matters. Growth is experienced as consciousness opens the path to progress. New information can keep your brain alert, keeping you feeling young and motivated. Your days will go by smoothly. Invest time to educate yourself so you can be ahead of the game of life.

Next, transforming all that information into a working plan that is useful for the improvement of your line of work is what is needed. Once the plan is carefully lined up, action is necessary to bring about the fruition of what was in the mind. What is intangible in the mind is given life and becomes tangible. The mind is like a factory. Use new information as the material to create a new product. The more information you have, the higher your chances of creating new products, and the higher the value you create for your services in your industry.

Use the worksheet at the end of this chapter to list negative thoughts you need to release, and the possibilities that will open up once they are released. Notice that the possibilities can go on and on. Feel free to use an extra sheet of paper to enumerate all the doors that will open up for you.

List negative thoughts that you need to release:

_____

_____

_____

_____

_____

_____

_____

_____

_____

List possibilities you can look forward to after releasing the limiting thoughts above:

_____

_____

_____

_____

_____

_____

_____

_____

_____

_____

_____

_____

# CHAPTER 5

## Happiness Is a State of Mind

Most folks are about as happy as they make
up their minds to be.

—*Abraham Lincoln*

Happiness is derived from within you. A lot of people think that happiness comes from their environment, but happiness is actually a decision that you make. It does not depend on the circumstance you are in. Happiness depends on your attitude toward life. You are solely responsible for your happiness. Blaming your unhappiness on others or on the circumstances of your life is like walking along the path of life blinded by darkness. Happiness is a choice of how you respond to the things that you experience. Your experiences change depending on the attitude you have chosen.

I once asked my friend Jane, "What makes you happy?" She answered that her shoes makes her happy. We both had a big laugh at that answer. Jane collected shoes of all styles and colors. According to her every morning when she gets herself ready for work, she looks at all her shoes, which number around 700 pairs stacked neatly on racks, and she admires them. She says the shoes make her feel good. Jane says they seem to jump out to her and say "Pick me, pick me!"

Then I asked Jane once again, "Jane what really makes you happy?" She became serious as she said that she feels good to be alive. She is grateful for each day; just getting up is awesome. Jane said that whenever she finds herself in a situation that does not feel right, she gets herself out of it quick. She said that awareness is the key. If a situation does not make her happy she gets out of it. If someone made her feel bad, she avoids that person. Jane takes initiative to avoid situations and people that can make her less happy. That, she said, is her secret to her happy state. Knowing when to stay in a situation and when to let go and move on.

You can be born in poverty and yet you can be happy. You can have tons of money and yet be unhappy. Meanwhile you can also be poor and miserable or rich and happy at the same time. Now that you know you have a choice, what situation would you rather be in? Would you choose to be rich and happy? When you are a happy rich person, you have more capacity to change the world to make it a better place. You can give to those who are suffering from hunger and disease. You can build hospitals for the terminally ill and provide decent housing for the elderly. You can support the causes you are passionate about. Your success and happiness will create a much-need change for people that are in need.

The Dalai Lama said, "If you want others to be happy, practice compassion. If you want to be happy, practice compassion."

## MAKE A DECISION TO BE HAPPY

Your happiness is not dependent on how people treat you; it is not dependent on the weather or the situation. Happiness depends solely on your attitude. You have the power to choose how to respond to people and situations. There are certain things in life that you can not control. Take, for example, the weather. Why make yourself upset about it, when you know in your heart that you can not control the weather?

## USE POSITIVE ATTITUDE

Glide through each day armed with positive attitude. Like anything, you can teach yourself to be happy and positive. Catch yourself when your mind is starting to sway toward negativity. Find the good in each human being you encounter, no matter where you are, and in every situation. When something is beyond your control, let it go and glide through the matter. It is not worth ruining your day over it. Being upset can raise your heartbeat and cause you unnecessary distress. Choose to stay calm, use positive attitude, and use your time constructively.

Time is precious. According to Charles Caleb Colton, "Time is the most undefinable yet paradoxical of things; the past is gone, the future is yet to come, and the present becomes the past even while we attempt to define it, and like the flash of lightning, at once exists and expires." Do not waste your time on things that defeat your true purpose in life. Dwelling on unhappiness is like building a wall too tall for you to see over between you and the better side of each moment. You lose your vision, feeling trapped in a world that you have created unconsciously for yourself.

## ARE YOU READY TO BE HAPPY?

The fact that you have picked up this book and read up to this point is a sign that you are ready to be happy. You are on your way to a true awakening of the spirit. You will free yourself from self-inflicted suffering by the knowledge of your power to choose. Use this power to drive positive life changes to enhance your happiness and success. You can start looking at the brighter side of any situation. Remember that the choice you make on how to respond to any person or situation is of grave importance in making your day a better day for you. Your decision to be happy affects the choices that you make. You can find happiness from within.

Take full responsibility for all your actions. No one else is responsible for your happiness but you. Try not to blame anyone for your unhappiness. You may have allowed yourself to be upset and be unhappy. It's good to know that you do have a choice.

## USE YOUR ENERGY FOR A GOOD CAUSE

Are there things or situations that make you unhappy? Have you taken the time to reflect on why these situations make you feel this way? Do you have the courage to face the issue to try to resolve it? Is it something you can change? Have you avoided confronting the issue? Is it fear that is stopping you? Do you feel that the agony of unhappiness has been prolonged by your inability to face the problem? Take action steps to change what you can to improve the way you feel. Face the problem squarely, and then do something to fix it. If the problem seems to be beyond your control, change your attitude. Changing your attitude toward something you cannot control can free you of unhappiness.

When it rains, be thankful for the water that nourishes the plants on earth. When the traffic is jammed, relax, be patient. Listen to some soothing music. It is useless to be frustrated about something that is beyond your control. Why waste energy unnecessarily by directing it toward something you cannot change? Save your energy, your fire, for something worthy of your time. Your days will be brighter. Every now and then there are days that are very trying. Try not to resort to focusing on the negative. The more focus is given to the pain, the deeper the suffering. Why suffer when you can control the way you feel by the way you think?

Consciously navigate the road of your daily journey with awareness that you have the power within you to be happy. The choice is yours. Live your life with the purpose of experiencing happiness and spreading happiness to all the people you encounter. Think good thoughts about people, even strangers. You are spreading good vibrations into the universe. Even when the physical eyes cannot see, the hearts of mankind can feel.

## YOU HAVE A CHOICE

You have the power to be happy. The circumstance of happiness is what you create by the power of choosing the attitude you conduct yourself with. Life unfolds by the choices you make. Let your choices unveil the light to shine stronger for you.

If you feel unhappy about your relationship, for example,

you can choose to truly work it out. Accept your partner unconditionally. Then go to a counselor for help. If you feel that it is hopeless, you do have a choice to move on. You can decide whether to suffer in an unhappy relationship or to go on your own to find love again. If you decide to stay, give it a hundred percent of what you've got. You can only get what you give out. The more you give, the more you get back. The rule of reciprocity works wonders.

Wake up the passion. You chose to be with this person because of all the wonderful qualities you saw in the beginning of your courtship. Focus on the good qualities of your partner. Write down all the great qualities that first attracted you to this person. Once on paper, you will realize how you have probably neglected to recognize and appreciate these qualities in the past few years.

Individuals need the approval of their partner, friends, and associates. Learn to give out sincere appreciation. Make it a habit to acknowledge others with a warm greeting and a smile. Voice your appreciation. When someone does something nice to you, be glad and verbally appreciate the kindness. When you see something good, appreciate with sincere words that can be uplifting.

When you decide to be happy, happiness will be a daily occurrence. People will notice your upbeat demeanor. People will feel good around you. Your presence will be a joy for your family, friends, associates, and strangers you encounter everyday.

## HOW TO FIND HAPPINESS

The foolish man seeks happiness in the
distance; the wise grows it under his feet.
—*James Oppenheim*

The sweetness of life, precious as gold, overflows from the heart. Fulfillment of the soul is derived from within. It comes from your inner being and manifests in your outer being. Make a decision to be happy. Happiness is a choice. Awareness of your full ability to enjoy a happy state can transform your attitude toward life.

Whatever you are doing in each of your present moments, immerse yourself in the task. Love your family. Love the people around you. Love life. Giving out love creates a foundation for happiness to surround you. Love and compassion that you give to your family and everyone that you come in contact with will give you joy. There is so much more contentment in the soul that gives. Grace in giving can enhance the happiness of the people around you and the happiness you experience inside.

Find the kind of work that expresses your passion in life. The harder you work, the more fun you experience. Joy at work can translate to peace within. When you have peace within, you have ease in getting along with the people around you and the flow of your daily activities can be smooth. You can decide to appreciate your work, fall in love with what you are doing each day. See the positive effect that your work can bring to others as well as to your life.

If you are very unhappy with your work, ask yourself why you are feeling this way, and then choose to find better opportunities that can give you fulfillment and happiness. Do not quit your job until you investigate well what is out there for you. Build a good resume that can sell your skills well. Send out your resume, but be careful to not send it to companies that deal with your present job, lest you risk losing your present job more quickly than you wanted. Be discreet until you are sure of what you want to do in the future. Find ways to acquire more skills to make you more attractive to prospective employers. No matter what you decide to do, make sure to find the work that best expresses your passion. Doing what you like frees the best within you, allowing for creativity to flow with total ease.

## STEPS TO TAKE TO HAVE A HAPPIER LIFE

These five steps will be discussed in more depth in later chapters.

• *Live a moment at a time.* Give value to every present moment; now is all that matters. When you learn to live for the moment, you give the best of what you can. You love with all your heart and cherish each moment that passes.

• *Be grateful.* A grateful heart is blessed. Live in constant gratitude for your life, health, family and friends. Appreciate your talents and abilities. Appreciate this wonderful universe that we live in. There is so much in life to be thankful for. Grace will continue to flow into your life.

• *Give love.* Give it out in abundance, wherever you are, whatever time of day. Give love to everyone who comes your

way. Have pleasant thoughts for others. Say a prayer
disabled stranger. Find a way to help others in anywa_
can throughout the day. Then greet people warmly.

• *Have a ready smile.* The love that you share through small
gestures to everyone all day can warm many hearts. In turn,
your heart grows with sweet joy.

• *Be forgiving.* A heart that holds grudges ceases to grow.
A hateful heart hardens like a rock. It becomes impossible for
a person with hateful heart to live a happy life. Forgiveness
releases tension that builds unnecessary hindrance to your
spiritual growth. Forgive that others may forgive you. No
one is perfect. Recognize that you have imperfections and
shortcomings as well. You have mistakes in the past that
hurt others. So why hold a grudge? Hatred is sickening and
debilitating, mentally and physically. Too much hatred can
make the mind and body deteriorate. Your negative thoughts
and hatred can cause you depression. The weakened mind
weakens the body. The immune system deteriorates as the
body weakens, making it susceptible to diseases. Forgive
and be free. Release the tension and let go of ill feelings.
Understand the imperfection of human nature. We tumble
and learn. Learn and let go, let your spirit grow.

# PART 2:

# Cultivating Positive Thoughts: Loving Life and Other People

CHAPTER 6

*Find Your Purpose*

Great minds have purposes, others have wishes.
—*Washington Irving*

Life is a precious journey to a person who has found the meaning of his or her existence. But for a person who remains in the dark about his or her purpose in life, living can be an exercise of moving through an endless confusing maze. Without direction, frustration is constant. Constant frustration can give way to anger or even depression. Why live in the dark? Find out why you are here. Find out how to make your life exciting and full of wonder.

My purpose in life is to help you and many others who are seeking to find success and happiness in life. I want to be able to awaken the awareness of many to enjoy life as it comes: one moment at a time.

### DISCOVER THE MEANING OF YOUR LIFE

Create a purposeful journey in life, so that you have a clear direction. Knowing the way can give you a clear sense of confidence. You do not need to be going through life aimlessly. Without proper direction, you can end up going in circles, getting nowhere, and wasting valuable time. Once you have unlocked the reason for your existence, you will find the significance of each moment that passes.

Take the time to reflect on how you can add value and meaning to the very precious gift of life that has been given to you. Ask yourself, "Why am I here? How can I use my time and creativity to help the people around me? How can I affect the people around me and the environment in the most positive way?"

Soon you will discover how much difference you can make to create a better world for you and the generations that will follow. Finding the meaning of your life can have a tremendous impact on how you see the world. It will look like a world full of resources for mankind to appreciate.

## KNOWING YOUR PURPOSE
## CAN GIVE YOU ENERGY

Once you know your purpose, you will not be lost. It is like finally having a map to guide you through. You will not be wasting time and energy driving on the road of life without proper direction. Instead, your focus will be on the important matter of getting to your destination. You will be able to enjoy the process of getting to where you want to be instead of worrying about getting lost. Living with a purpose creates a positive focal point that generates energy from within. It dramatically increases your energy, giving you more power to mold your environment. Energy can take your sleeping potential and make it come to life, giving you the power to help others around you.

Living in awareness of the value of each moment helps you find purpose to:

Love

Grow

Learn

Meditate and reflect on your life. Write down your life purpose.

_____

_____

_____

_____

_____

_____

_____

_____

_____

_____

_____

_____

_____

_____

_____

_____

_____

_____

_____

# CHAPTER 7

## *Living Life to the Fullest*

Living life to the fullest is living in total awareness of how we affect others and our surroundings. Your cup must continuously overflow to share with those around you. Your kindness is like water and fertilizer that moisten the soil and provide nourishment to seeds that they may sprout in abundance. As each plant in the garden grows, it carries a part of what you have given it in each of its cells. Likewise, your acts of kindness are recorded in the hearts of the grateful people you have touched.

### GIVE A PART OF YOUR SELF

Self is lost in the totality of the general goodness of the whole. When you work for the general goodness, you become a part of something bigger. The power of the mass is stronger than a mere individual. Giving of your self adds positive energy for a greater common good that elevates the quality of the lives of more people. A group of people sharing what they have to enrich others who have less than themselves makes a difference, not only to those at the receiving end but to those who are giving as well.

When life is full of meaning, each moment filled with love, there is no time for self-absorption. Feelings of emptiness and self-pity will be replaced with true compassion and concern for the welfare of others. There will only be time for jubilation: each moment calls for a celebration.

A sense of completeness that is derived from the choices that you make can lead you to fulfill your life purpose. Living in full awareness of the now can help in making sure that you use each precious moment to create happiness for you and the people around you. Happiness is intoxicating and contagious. Choose to live a happy life. Everyone has the capacity to be happy. Happiness comes from within.

Your constant compassion for others increases your ability to make someone happy. Seeing someone happy increases the joy that you feel inside. This creates a constant cycle of a life lived in the expression of love and kindness, in which you can find true fulfillment.

Indulge yourself in each moment that passes; each moment is a chance to make a difference in the world, which is so full of opportunities to help others. Helping in small ways every day creates a habit of being filled with kindness and love. The more you give of yourself, the more you find purpose in each step that you make; each step becomes a meaningful passage in your journey in life. Happiness is experienced within the process, not before or after. Be present for each moment, so that you may experience the true value of the purpose behind every action. Live and feel the fun. Life is a fun-filled gift. Every day is a wrapped bowl full of surprises. Unwrap each day with the eagerness of a child, looking forward to interacting with your family, friends, and even strangers. Count the many faces that lights up from the love that you give; the radiance that engulfs your soul is priceless.

## EXPRESS LOVE

Express your love openly. I enjoy professing my love to my family. I hug my son a few times a day, telling him how much I love him. Not a day passes without me telling my husband that I love and care for him. I kiss and hug my mother often, telling her how much I appreciate what she does for me. My mother lives with us and has helped me in the care of my son since he was young, especially when I started flying for a living. My mother is a soothing presence in our lives. I am so fortunate to have a wonderful loving mother.

Hug your loved ones as often as you can. Notice how animals are affectionate with their young. The cat nurtures her little kittens while the dog nurtures and plays with her puppies. Growing up in the Philippines as a child, I had a cat named Ngawpat. Ngawpat was given to me as a gift when I was five years old. She was a very clever cat. Ngawpat found a mate and had little kittens. I was amazed how Ngawpat took care of her young. One day, one kitten disappeared. It must have wandered into the woods behind my house. It took one week before the little kitten found its way home. My whole family witnessed the homecoming, but it was not a happy one. Ngawpat scolded the little kitten for hours, just like a human mother would do if a child had not returned home in a long time. My mother, brother, and I laughed in disbelief watching the commotion between the cat and her kitten. Ngawpat smacked the kitten with her paws many times as if giving her young one some lessons. After an hour or so, however, the cat and the kitten made up and there was much affection once again.

Humankind, as rational as we are, lost the touch of showing affection openly. We are too busy living in our own world of self-absorption. We worry so much about our problems and ourselves, our next meal, and how we can pay our bills that we lose touch of what is important in our day-to-day life. What is important is your family, friends, and all the people around you. Use quality time to spend with them to show them love and care. You might be wondering why I include all the people around as part of what is important. Everyone is important, because the existence of others is a chance for us to share the abundance of what we have. What we have inside is an ocean of love, a love that extends without limitation, a love that bind us together. Sharing what we have allows us to grow. Growing is a part of living. Every one of us is a part of a whole connected universe.

No matter what race, color, weight, or shape, we are all brothers and sisters. Compassion of the human spirit unifies the human race. Treat others the way you want them to treat you in your daily life. It is the rule of the selfless to love and accept others no matter how different they may seem on the outside. We are all one in the spirit.

## COMPASSION IS MAGICAL

What is compassion? Why do we need compassion to achieve success and happiness now that we may live life to the fullest? Compassion is your deep connection to the feelings and need of others. It is recognizing, as well as sympathizing with, what emotions other people may be experiencing, as you might if you picture yourself in their situation. Being in touch at this deeper level as you interact with people makes you consider their feelings. It is the human antenna, guiding your actions appropriately as you navigate through life, and it strengthens your connectivity with your family and everyone else.

Each human existence is connected to all life forces. You are a part of the main life source that created the universe, therefore you and me and all the life that surrounds us are related. Treat everyone around you like a son, daughter, brother, sister, mother, or father. Looking at another person from a perspective of blood relation allows you to treat them with utmost compassion. Compassionate existence is full of purpose. It can bring you inner fulfillment. Make it a purpose to give love in each moment that you have, learning and growing from each experience. Out of your compassion for others spring kindness and generosity. These are golden attributes of a person who is destined to succeed.

Bring people up with you as you strive to live fully, developing your gifts as well as the talents of those who surround you. The quality of the relationships you create gives you an advantage due to the solid support system you have built. You have people you can count on when you need advice or help on any issues. Your compassion, kindness, and generosity will build a network of reliable connections.

Generosity opens the gate to unlimited abundance in all facets of life. A heart that gives is selfless. Living your life selflessly in each moment is living in an enlightened way. It is living in the awareness that each individual is foremost a soul, and then a physical being as the secondary structure. Souls, which are eternal from God had been given the gift of physical temporal life on earth, have boundless capacity to love. Love binds us to all existence through our compassionate choices, endearing actions, and kind considerations. The more you feel connected the more you have peace of mind. The more peace of mind you have, the more fulfilling life is. Happiness is achieved in a heart full of energy for life.

Each activity becomes an opportunity to expand love. Joy is a constant companion when you live in a circle of connectivity. Strengthen your connection to others through your sincere compassionate awareness of the needs of others. Your kindness will reward you with a lightness of heart.

This lifetime is precious, live it to the fullest. Don't waste any time regretting what you could have done differently. Today you can have a fresh start to do what you want with your life. It is never too late to start evaluating what you can do to improve on what you have. Start utilizing a total command of your mind to cultivate positive thoughts for success. Live life with a purpose. Keep purposes alive using positive verbal affirmations and positive visual imagery. Life will be so much more fun to experience. Each moment becomes a chance to progress to a higher level of existence spiritually, physically, and financially.

## OVERCOME YOUR PAST

Dare to be different. You do not have to conform to everyone's expectations of you. Excel in what you do best. Find your true strengths, then compete with your best. Compete only with yourself. It is good to shine, rising above everyone's expectations.

Some people grew up with negative influences around them. Being told as a child, "You will not amount to anything, you can't do anything right," can have a psychological impact on a child, especially if the negative comments are repeated throughout the early stages of life. If you are someone who was subjected to such negative verbal abuse as a child, it is important to let go of the past and forgive those who have wronged you. As an adult, recognize how the past affected you, then get some help.

Live for today, because today is fresh, and you can create a new beginning. Any past experiences that can bring out painful emotions can be dealt with by recognizing that they are there and that you are capable of letting them go. To do this, some people choose to vent their emotions with their close friends. Others may choose therapy. After you have done what is best for you, try to bury the negative emotions of the past and refrain from unearthing them over and over. Overcoming adversities has strengthened you.

Some people are very lucky to have grown up around very positive parents who encouraged them to believe in themselves and do their best. These lucky individuals have a greater chance of growing up confident and excelling in their work and their personal relationships.

If you are not among the lucky ones who grew up with great parents, now that you are an adult, break free from the limitations that have been embedded in your mind from your youth. Understand that you have the same chance in succeeding as anyone, depending on how you perceive yourself. It does not matter what your past may be. Find a mentor who can guide you in the right direction.

# CHAPTER 8

## Living to Love and Grow

Helping others in any way can bring you a lot of fulfillment and happiness. The more people you help, the more happiness you feel within. Focus your life for the good of others. It is the most heart-warming way to live. You have a lot of gifts to give, and you can create a magical experience for others with your kindness and compassion. What is in your heart is an unlimited capacity to make another person feel better. No one should ever feel alone. We all belong to each other. Spread love like the birds spread the seeds in the garden of the earth.

Love is a gift that you can give in abundance to all the people that you meet each day. It is a matter of having good intention in your heart for all. Small gestures of love that you share with others will uplift your heart throughout the day, adding sweetness and inspiration to a day that may have been full of emptiness and sadness. A smile can go a long way. A sincere greeting can lift a soul.

The interactions we have with our family, friends, and associates join together to allow wisdom and love to grow. Every morning as you wake up, celebrate the new day as a day that will bring forth new opportunities. Expect wonderful things to come your way. Believe that each moment of the day has a purpose that contributes to your growth. Life is a constant learning process; a new lesson emerges in every turn. At each one, ask yourself, "What can I learn from this?" Cherish the new information. What you learn can make you strong. New knowledge can make you alert. As long as you live, keep on learning. Successful people continuously accumulate information as they navigate their journey in life. Cultivate a hunger for new knowledge everyday. You will see the difference in the direction that your life will take you.

## HELPING OTHERS INCREASES YOUR CONFIDENCE

Make yourself useful. There are countless of opportunities throughout the day to help others. The more helpful you are toward your neighbor, the better you feel about yourself. Think of the grateful hearts and the sweet loving smiles that will surround you. Start with simple acts of kindness, consistently exercising helpfulness and kindness each chance that you get. After a while, these traits will become a part of your personality.

> Everytime you smile at someone, it is
> an action of love, a gift to that person, a
> beautiful thing.
>> —*Mother Theresa*

Smile, smile, smile. It is so pleasant to see a joyous face. Your ready smile warms the people around you. Greet people cheerfully wherever you are. Your happy upbeat demeanor can start you at a good pace. Radiance shines out from a heart full of kindness and love. Love is felt without words. It overflows through the pores of any face that holds a sincere smile, lifting onlooking spirits in joy.

Living life with a purpose makes you conscious of the needs of others. Filling those needs, through small to great acts of kindness, allows you to find deeper meaning in your existence. For instance, when you see an elderly person trying to cross the street, choose to lend a hand instead of just continuing on with what you are doing. When you happen to look out the window on a winter day and see your eighty-year-old neighbor shoveling the driveway, step out there to do it yourself. A deep awareness of being connected to others will allow you to see the elderly person as if he or she were your mother or father.

When a friend is in an emotional distress, sometimes all you have to do is be there to support. Let your friend get it off her chest, whatever is bottled within. Then encourage your friend to let it go. Healing of the pain can start immediately after the letting go process.

Use each moment as an opportunity to express love through your actions. As you practice kind acts, a genuine compassion for others will become a core of your daily life. Having a loving intent behind your actions of kindness will open up your life to the grace of abundance.

## A PURPOSE FULFILLED IN EACH MOMENT

These simple acts of kindness may not seem like much, but they can surely make a difference in someone's day. Positive attitude and heartfelt action will instill in you a purpose that can be fulfilled in each moment. Create a loving relationship with mankind and nature. There are many opportunities for all of us to affect others positively. Helping others can make you feel good about yourself. Your self-esteem will continue to soar. You will start finding purpose in things that used to be routine. Life will take on a new meaning.

Give freely of your self without expectation. Reward is felt within the heart. There is so much joy in a life dedicated to serving and helping others. Human existence is so rich with opportunities to make a difference. Let your lifetime count. Having a pure, well-meaning intention behind your every action can uplift another human being. Your actions do not have to be grand: a trickle of kindness from you throughout the day will still elevate the spirit of others.

Helping others allows your soul to grow. You become a more grounded person with an enhanced sense of self. It enriches your life with love and priceless joy. Think less of your own needs and think more of what you can do to bring people up with you. Share your wisdom, share your time, and share your love and what you have. What you have acquired by the end of your earthly life is not as important as what you have given of yourself to make a difference in the world you will one day leave behind.

## BECOME A POSITIVE ENERGY FORCE

When you are continuously contributing to the good of others, you create a positive vibrating energy that warms the people you encounter. You become an irresistible presence. The pleasure of your company will energize any room you occupy. Living with a purpose makes your daily life flow like a stream. The abundance of grace you encounter will be tremendous, and your personality will start attracting great possibilities that can open doors to new beginnings.

## A GRATEFUL HEART HAS MANY BLESSINGS

Immerse yourself in total gratitude. Live each moment in complete awareness and savor the priceless value of your time. Bring to life the best of your abilities. The value of your time increases as your growing awareness expands, elevating the awesome gift of your life. Time is gold. Waste your time and as such waste your life. What a shame to be breathing and yet not living. How foolish to not partake in the adventure of a happy life. There is so much you can do for yourself and for others, as well as for your environment. Look at each moment as an opportunity to exercise selflessness, thereby improving your inner fulfillment, affecting others in a positive way, and at the same time improving the world around you.

To be happy, start counting your blessings throughout the day. Be grateful for the gift of life. Be thankful for the fact that you are able to get up this morning. Cherish the health of your mind and body. Be glad for the roof over your head, the food that you eat each day to nourish your body, and the water that you drink. Take the time to appreciate your partner in life. Give thanks for your children and the happiness they give you with their loving smiles and inquisitive questions. Give thanks for your job and the income it generates to take care of you and your family.

Celebrate your freedom: living in a free country has been taken for granted by many people. Cherish your ability to make your own choices. You can elect the officials that you want to run your country. You can choose to work for a company or work for yourself. You can choose a mediocre neighborhood to live in or you can choose to be ambitious and work wiser to afford a better lifestyle. You can choose positive thoughts over negative thoughts after you have educated yourself with the power of your mind to change your environment.

No matter what your situation is in life, there are hundreds of things to be thankful for. Get a pen and a paper (or use the worksheet at the end of this chapter) and write down all the things that you can be thankful for. Write as many as you can find. Use some quiet moments to reflect on your list. Read your notes every morning when you get up, so that you may start your day with a better attitude. Carry the notes with you in your wallet or bag so that you can access and review them anytime, especially when negativities starts to creep into your mind.

It is a challenge to remember the blessings that we have in our possession when some people around us have made it a habit to spend their days expressing dissatisfaction of what they have or what they do not have in life. This type of negative unloading conversation seems to be the norm in our society. That is why keeping a record of your blessings is a key to remind yourself of how lucky you are to be alive. Counting your blessings can keep your mind on the right track. Your attitude becomes congruent with your inner disposition of peace. When you feel blessed, you feel good inside; when you feel good inside, you are at peace; when you have inner peace, it radiates into your surroundings.

Keep in mind that there are other people who may have less than what you have; they may not even have freedom, depending in which country they reside. Share what you can to uplift the lives of people who may need shelter, food, and medicine. Actions of generosity are the best expressions of gratitude.

I am grateful for:

1. _____

2. _____

3. _____

4. _____

5. _____

6. _____

7. _____

8. _____

9. _____

10. _____

# CHAPTER 9

## Using the Rule of "Karma" for Your Personal Life and Business

"Karma" is derived from Hinduism and Buddhism. The dictionary interprets it as action that brings upon oneself results, good or bad, that are similar to the results one caused. In other words, "Do unto others as you want others to do unto you."

### BE AWARE OF THE FEELINGS OF OTHERS

Ask yourself, "How would I feel if I were in their shoes?" Literally imagine yourself being in the position of the other person you are interacting with. How do you want to be treated? How will you react in receiving an act of kindness from someone? How will you feel when someone treats you with disrespect? When you treat someone in a manner that destroys the flow of fluid positive energy, you are breaking the link of love that binds each human existence.

Happiness can be experienced in your daily interaction with people. Hurting anyone in any manner can in turn hurt you as well. Remember to find something good in each person you encounter. Each individual has a soul from God that is basically good. Treat people kindly and respectfully. Treating others the way you want them to treat you is a very good way to enhance the quality of your relationships. If you want peace at home and at work, conduct yourself in a way that radiates peace. If you long to be loved, give out as much love as you can to the people that you encounter everyday. Love can be a simple act of saying something nice to someone, acknowledging people with a simple smile and a warm hello. Or it could be an offer of some help to someone by giving advice. It is easier to give love than to withhold it. You can experience the release of that great energy within you and share it with someone, making the other person feel special and fuller after your interaction with them. Each day becomes a day full of chances to uplift another human being, chances to love and chances to be compassionate. When you take these chances, you become a gentler and kinder human being.

## FAIRNESS IS THE KEY

Treat others with fairness. If you do, people will look at you as someone who is looking out for their best interests. Being fair is the opposite of being greedy. Greed can destroy relationships. If you want people to trust you, show them that you are not taking advantage of them, whether in your business dealings or in your personal relationships.

In what position can you put yourself so that both parties can take something good out of the situation? Is it possible for both parties to feel good? Your family and associates will become more loyal to you when they know you are sincerely taking into consideration what is good for all. Your home life will flourish. At work, your fairness will encourage creativity. A positive atmosphere is conducive to the development of a state of well-being for all the people you work with. A happier group of people can work better as a team. A team has more power than a lone worker.

## DO THE RIGHT THING

Think before you act, think before you utter your words. Be vigilant about always doing the right thing. Action can cause happiness or pain. Let your actions speak what is in your heart. The wholeness of your thoughts and intentions before an act is vital to the execution of what is right. Choose to let happiness be your guide, the meter of your intuition. How would you feel if you were the receiver of the words that you are about to say? Can the words that you are about to say add to the happiness of the other person? Words can either warm a heart or put a dagger through it.

The words that you release cannot be retrieved back, so be careful to choose your words wisely. Have you ever been in a situation where you have just uttered something so damaging or embarrassing that you wish you thought better? You wished to take those words back, but it was too late. Words are powerful. Let your words become a fountain of love and knowledge. Refer to chapter 28 for more about why the choice of words is important for success and happiness.

## ACTIONS INTERPRET YOUR THOUGHTS

Your good intentions will become apparent in your daily activities. Kind thoughts will materialize as respectful kind actions. The way people react to you is a reflection of your own character. Love begets love, as kindness begets kindness. If you treat someone with spite, what reaction do you think will you get? If, in the midst of fury, you say something harsh and painful, how do you think the other person will feel? Even if you think you are right and they are wrong, is it worth aggravating the situation by hurting the other person more? Giving pain to someone will increase your negative "karma."

Increase your positive "karma" instead in your daily life and business by giving out positive energy through your thoughts, words, and actions. It is a single and yet powerful tool in improving the quality of your relationships. Your personal life will greatly improve. It can also elevate your productive interaction with people at work.

To effectively use the "Rule of Karma" follow these steps:
1. Treat people the way you want them to treat you.
2. Think before you act.
3. Use words carefully and lovingly.
4. Work with good intention.

What changes can you make in the way you treat your family in order for the rule of "karma" to work for you at home?

1. _____

2. _____

3. _____

4. _____

5. _____

6. _____

7. _____

8. _____

9. _____

10. _____


How can you treat your colleagues, customers, and strangers to make the rule of "karma" work for you in your work life?

1. _____

2. _____

3. _____

4. _____

5. _____

6. _____

7. _____

8. _____

9. _____

10. _____

# Enjoy Life

Humor has a way of bringing people together. It unites people. In fact, I'm rather serious when I suggest that someone should plant a few Whoopee Cushions in the United Nations.

—*Ron Dentinger*

## USE HUMOR

To become successful and happy now in your life you need to be able to take things lightly with some humor. It is a good way of breaking the ice. It is so delightful to be around people with great sense of humor. Humor is a fun way of connecting with others in an upbeat energizing atmosphere. It lightens up moods and makes everyone feel good. Things seem to flow with ease, and stress diminishes. Communication increases with a graceful flow when humor is employed.

The more you laugh, the more you enjoy living life. Laughter is contagious. It tickles the senses with delight. It gives you a feeling of lightness in your heart that makes you free. When you laugh often, tensions dissipate and are replaced with freedom to enjoy life. Laughter has a mysterious way of easing your pain and helping you forget your sorrows. It elevates your mental state, allowing you to feel euphoric about life. It reminds you that it is good to be alive. Your attitude toward life becomes more positive, because a life full of laughter is fun. Life is like a game played by those who conquer all difficulties armed with the techniques of true happiness, one of which is humor.

So add humor into your day. Laugh heartily at yourself and at your silly mistakes.

A friend named Eric who works with me relayed to me this story. When Eric was about four years old, he used to go with his mother to the store to shop. His mom would put him in the cart while picking up the goods that the family needed. Pointing to the box of Kotex pads, Eric wanted to know what it was used for. His mother replied that it was a box of bandages. But Eric wondered why his mom kept buying the packages every month when he had not seen anyone getting hurt that often at home.

One day, while Eric was playing with his toy cars outside the house, the mailman named Mike came to deliver the mail. While walking up the stairs towards the house, Mike stumbled and hurt his right knee, which began to bleed. Eric witnessed the fall, and told Mike not to worry because inside the bathroom there was a huge box of bandages. He told the mailman to wait as he rushed into the house. Eric came out of the house with two Kotex pads. He proceeded to take the cover off the sticky strip from the back of the pad and stuck it on Mike's injured knee. Mike did not know what to say. He wanted to laugh, but instead asked Eric if his mother was home. Eric's mother appeared at the front door with a horrified look on her face. She had a few short words with mailman Mike, and he turned and went on his way.

Later that evening she decided to tell the truth to her little son about the purpose of Kotex pads. The next day when Eric went to school he told his teacher, "Do you believe that my mom actually sticks this big bandage up her butt? Do you do that too?" The teacher immediately contacted Eric's mother.

Mailman Mike became a good friend. For years, every time Mike delivered the mail, he never ceased to ask Eric for a bandage. They would have a big laugh about it. Mike has just recently retired from the postal service. To this day, when family gathers together, Eric's mom tells the story over and over to anyone who would listen. It never ceases to break the ice.

The moral of Eric's story is; do not take things too seriously unless you want to grow old quickly. Stay young forever with humor. When you are happy it shows. Your joyous glow of energy gives out positive vibrations. People become naturally drawn to you. You will enjoy life with awesome euphoric zest.

## EXPERIENCE NATURE

Imagine walking in a winding path in the midst of a vast wooden area. The wind brushing against your skin whistles a tune that blends with the rustling of the leaves, creating rhythmic music and circulating the sweet scent of the flowers. Your eyes take in the magnificent beauty of the blue sky that stretches over the valleys and the mountains that stand with pride. The scene's soothing delight is magnified in your soul with total abandon. Your heart explodes with joy.

Every now and again take a break from your busy schedule and set a time to be with nature. Feel your connection to the rest of creation. Take the time to appreciate its splendor. Soak your senses in its beauty. Nature has a way of clearing your thoughts. You are a part of this masterpiece. The more you feel that you are a part of a whole, the more naturally you will respect nature and the people around you. Learning to respect your environment as well as people you encounter is very nourishing to the soul. We are a part of a great universe that in so many ways influences us as we in turn influence it. What we do toward people, things, and nature can affect us whether we like it or not.

Think with this respect in mind before you act. Putting good intention behind every action will allow you to enjoy nature and enjoy life to the fullest.

# Forgiveness: Freedom From the Bondage of Anger and Pain

To forgive is to set a prisoner free and
discover that the prisoner was you.

*—Lewis B. Smedes*

To forgive is a virtue of the soul. Forgiving is the beginning of healing. It is a way of moving on. Storing anger and resentment within you is like storing lethal toxins in your body that can harm not only your physical composition but your soul as well. Deep anger can kill you. Your health is greatly affected by the condition of your emotions and your state of mind. A happier individual will live a longer, higher quality life. A constantly angry person will one day find himself or herself alone and possibly ill. No one wants to hang around a person who finds a reason to be angry at any given opportunity.

Exercise patience. The hyper schedules that we commit ourselves to can make us lose sight of what is important in our lives. Peaceful compassionate relationships must be upheld. Be forgiving and let go of ill feelings. It is not worth your time and effort to waste your emotions on something as destructive as anger. You will become a healthier, happier person when you are able to forgive. Experience loyal, lasting friendships with people you care for. Your family and friends are your anchor; let them enjoy your warm upbeat presence.

Allow me to tell you how I learned to forgive. When I was a child, my mother taught my brother and me to love even our own enemy. Mother told us to pray for anyone who causes us pain. She showed us how to forgive, setting examples for us as we grew up. She is a loving person who defused anger by her calmness in the midst of turmoil.

I was born and raised in the Philippines. When I was nine years old and my brother Sunny was twelve, we were renting a small store space from my Uncle Pete (my mother's oldest brother). Uncle Pete was married to Aunt Rose. They had five children. All of them lived in the second floor of the house. Our "sari-sari" (convenience) store was located at the front area of the house. Students who went to medical and nursing school within the area rented the first floor right behind the store.

My Aunt Rose had the most ferocious temper. She pestered people around her on a daily basis, especially her husband, my poor Uncle Pete. Uncle Pete was the target of constant verbal abuse by his own wife. Aunt Rose was often looking for confrontations. One day, she started accusing my mother of not paying rent for the store. It was a big fat lie. Uncle Pete and Aunt Rose together with their five children took the groceries from our store on credit for most of their daily consumption. Whatever merchandise— such as bread, canned goods, rice, and soda—the family took from our store was signed for by the family member who took it. The list was long. At the end of every month, my mother tallied all the debt, and deducted our rent from it for the new month.

Aunt Rose constantly screamed the nastiest profanities at my mother, my brother, and me. She was adept at all the profanities in the book. She screamed with all her might to humiliate us in front of anyone listening. Mind you, neighbors could hear her within a two-block radius because she happened to be so vocally gifted. She should have been an opera singer.

Aunt Rose took Mom, my brother, and I to court over her accusations of unpaid rent for the store space we were occupying at that time. I can still remember going to court once a month for many years. The law system in the Philippines can be very slow. I dreaded those court appearances. I often spoke on behalf of my family, as young as I was. I defended my mother. The case dragged on for many years, like a dark cloud hovering over our heads. A court-appointed lawyer defended us for free. My family was not in a position to afford the expenses. It was a nightmare.

But throughout the ordeal, my mother never lost control. Whenever she started to hear Aunt Rose scream profanities by the store, she would either start singing some religious songs loudly or she would turn the radio loud to her favorite program to counter the screams. My mother never screamed back at my Aunt Rose. Mother went to the lengths of demanding that my brother and I show Aunt Rose respect. We had to greet Aunt Rose every time we saw her on the street, despite of how harsh and abusive she was to our family. My mother told us to show our Aunt Rose respect. We had to bow and touch the back of Aunt Rose's hand to our forehead. This type of greeting is part of the custom in the Filipino culture, a way of showing respect to elderly people. Can you imagine bowing your head and taking the hand of a serpent like enemy? Oh, it was difficult. But obedient kids that we were, we obeyed our mother's order. We even got used to it. Aunt Rose even managed to smile at us every now and then when we showed our respect.

All in all it taught my brother and me the value of forgiveness. To this day, I do not hold grudges toward others. Grudges can eat away your soul. Forgiving lightens the burden of the heart. There is freedom in letting go. It showed us that no matter what, you can love even those who are a challenge to love. We learned to love the person even as we despise her actions.

My mother eventually won the case when I was in my mid-twenties and already residing in America. She invited Aunt Rose to her "farewell party" when she was getting ready to come to America. They had a great time. I think my Aunt Rose was puzzled and amazed by the kindness of my mother. My mother is an incredible woman. She treated her enemy with love and kindness even after many years of abuse. My brother and I were the biggest winners because we learned such an important lesson at a very young, tender age.

## FORGIVING AND MOVING ON

Let the past be in the past where it belongs. Bury unpleasant memories in the dust. Living in the past will hinder you from moving forward. If you keep looking behind you, you will lose sight of what is in front of you, making you stumble in your journey. Leave unhappy memories behind: they can only drain you of energy that you need. Bringing old painful emotions into the present can make you relive the negative emotions. Keep your eyes forward, and savor the essence of the present moment. This very moment is the most important moment of your life. Focus your mind, heart, and sight on the present. How you live this moment will ensure you of a better tomorrow if you are wise enough to spend it well. Today is a fresh start. You can build a life of happiness and success through your disciplined thoughts. Make every step create a better memory for you.

Forgiving frees your mind, body, and soul from the negative constriction of anger and pain. It opens up a lot of space for more creativity to do more positive things. You gain strength in character as you learn to love even the most difficult one to love. Overall, the reward of peace is priceless. Peace is the jewel inside of you. Guard it, protect it, and be in tune with it.

Forgiving:
- Frees your soul
- Opens space for creativity
- Enables you to love your enemy
- Gives you peace

# CHAPTER 12

# Rule Your Emotions

Emotions are feelings within us that affect us psychologically and physically if we allow them to. Emotions can only have power over you when you allow them to overwhelm you. You have the freedom of choice to decide what you allow to occupy your mind and body. Your true essence is separate from your emotions. You can choose to release negative emotions out of your system. Storing negative emotions within you can affect you mentally and physically. Remember that you have the power to control what goes on inside your mind. The choice is in your hands.

To live more happily, you need to live in consciousness of the fact that what happens within you and the feelings you are experiencing are derived from what you have allowed to dwell in your precious mind and body. Remember that your thoughts can affect your physical state. You are not forced by anyone to feel the way you do. You can choose to eliminate what limiting emotions you are experiencing. You can do this through a conscious decision to live in awareness of your capacity to rule your emotions. Your emotions are not attached to you. They are totally separate from your being. You become stronger and happier when you become in control of your emotions.

There are positive emotions such as courage, acceptance, and peace. These emotions give you increased energy, love, and selflessness. Indulge yourself with these feelings. They can give you a happy, upbeat attitude toward life. Celebrate each breath that you take in gratitude. Live each moment in total awareness. Life will be a heck of a ride.

On the other hand, there are limiting emotions such as anger, pride, grief, lust, fear, and apathy. These emotions can hurt you if you allow them to run your life. Be aware that you have the power to let these emotions go. If you find this particularly difficult, I suggest that you check out *The Sedona Method* by Hale Dowskin. It walks you step-by-step through the whole process of releasing these emotions that can bring you down.

You might be thinking that releasing negative emotion is easy to say but hard to do. I agree with you: it is difficult in the beginning, but constant practice will make you better at letting go. Then it just comes so naturally, it becomes a part of how you live your life.

Take, for instance, grief. An example is the loss of a loved one. We mourn for our loss. Allow the tears to fall: they are like water from heaven that release and ease the pain. I can still remember when my father died in the arms of my mother. My parents had been separated for 21 years. My dad was an alcoholic and was not very nice to my mother. My mother raised my brother and I alone without any help from my father. As I prepared to send for my mother to come to America, she informed me that she would bring my father along and that I must send for my father as well. After their many years of separation, I wondered why my mother wanted to bring my father. She said that it was a dream of my dad to be able to come to the States. I obeyed my mother.

Meanwhile, my mom did not know his whereabouts. She embarked on a search and called many relatives to find out where he might be. She eventually found him in one of his relatives' homes, very drunk. She got him cleaned up and told him that she was taking him to America. They arrived in New York in 1996. Within a year, he was diagnosed with lung cancer. He had smoked since he was 14 years old; he tried to quit many times but he never succeeded. He tried to conceal it from us in the beginning, so by the time the family found out about the cancer, it had spread throughout his body.

My mother took care of him lovingly, taking him to all his doctor's appointments and radiation treatments. She fed him when he could no longer feed himself. My father clung to her for her courage. Amazingly, my father was able to walk even to his last days. He lost his voice, resorting to hand signals. He practically followed my mother all over the house. I believe he was afraid to die alone. Every night, they would pray together. My mother would sit or kneel down to pray while my dad would lie down beside her. He followed her with his mind as she said her prayers aloud because he was no longer able to speak. On my father's last day, my brother Sunny arrived from San Diego to be with us. That evening, as my father sat in the living room, I remembered telling him how wonderful it was for us to finally all be under one roof after 21 years. My dad was sitting in the couch, and our eyes met. I smiled at him and he smiled back with a happy glitter in his eyes. Then dad gave a thumbs-up.

In the middle of the night, my father walked into the room occupied by my brother. He pointed to the morphine patch on his chest. He wanted another patch, gesturing that he was in pain. The next morning, my father died while my mother gave him a sponge bath. I can still remember my mother's cry, calling my father over and over: "Pang, Pang, Pang" (a slang for Papa that she used to call him). My brother and I rose from our sleep and we sobbed and cried.

It is sad for any family to experience a loss of a loved one. The tremendous love and support from our relatives and friends helped us in those moments. Remember that the soul lives forever.

Now let us talk about fear. Fear is experienced when a person is afraid of an imaginary outcome. It can trap you and stagnate you. Fear of taking a chance in improving your present life, for example, needs to be reevaluated in terms of the real risks and benefits. Conquer fear with courage and knowledge. Develop a strategy that enables you to see beyond the fear of the action. Instead, weigh what the outcome can actually bring you. Tasting the sweetness of the fruit is better than dwelling in the midst of fear. Living in constant fear of change can only give you regrets. In the end it can eventually make you angry with yourself for all the lost opportunities and the lost time.

September 11th 2001, was a very personal experience for me that mixed both grief and fear. I was still a single mother living in the Pittsburgh area. As a reserve flight attendant, I had to work aggressively to make ends meet. That meant working on my days off and most of the holidays. September

11th was my day off, but I gave it up to make it possible for me to get more time in. When a flight attendant is on reserve, the airline will pay him or her a minimum pay whether he or she flies or not. However, it does not amount to much for a single income household with three mouths to feed. So I worked back-to-back trips because I wanted to take good care of my son and my mother and I wanted to save money to buy a house of my own. I was constantly packing my bag, even as I arrived home from a trip. I was exhausted at times. I even nodded off driving home from six days straight of flying, an average of fifteen flights. But I kept on working. I knew exactly what I wanted and I went out to get it. I wanted a house very badly. I became more careful after nodding off while driving. I made sure not to turn on the television when I got into my hotel room in the evenings. What a difference a few hours sleep made.

On that morning of September 11th, I remember being in such a great mood. I usually would welcome the passengers into the airplane with a big smile. I would say, "Welcome aboard! Welcome to my living room!" (I would wink as the passengers laugh). I would sometimes say, "This is the party flight, come on in." I love to make people laugh. The flight went smoothly. I worked with two other flight attendants who also had good senses of humor. After we finished the service we chatted and exchanged jokes and laughed, not knowing what had happened. As we landed and taxied on the runway of Tampa Florida airport, the pilot made an announcement that the country was in a state of emergency. I cannot recall word for word what the captain said, but as we stopped he opened the door to the cockpit and called in the lead flight attendant to inform us of what was going on. The captain did not want us to panic while we were in flight, choosing to let us know on the ground. It took a while before we secured a gate, as every aircraft was commanded to land. When we were eventually able to deplane, we were stunned as we stared at the television showing the airplanes crashing into the Twin Towers one after the other. All I kept asking was "Why? Why would anyone do such an evil act? Why would people kill themselves and kill thousands of others with them?" Initially I was in total disbelief and shock. We were told to proceed to the hotel until the company figured out what we needed to do. Many flight attendants went home, opting to drive from Florida.

As for myself, I felt relieved when I was finally able to reach my loved ones to assure them that I was OK. Everybody in my immediate family was frantic. Cell phone towers were jammed with so many calls that it took a long time to get through. My mother told me that my brother Sunny called to ask her where I was. All that my mother could say was that I started a trip but that she did not have a clue where I was going. Mother described how my brother broke down and cried on the phone. I normally don't tell my mother the details of my trips. What I usually end up saying before I get out of the door is that I have a four-day trip, I will be back on this particular day, and that I will call in between flights as well as when I get to my overnight. Once in a while I would tell my mom what exciting city I would be in when I like a particular destination. I was dating my current husband at that time; he was in the air as well on another aircraft. He traveled four days a week and went back home on weekends to spend time with his children. We finally got hold of each other and were glad to hear each other's voice.

No one could have predicted what happened that morning. I opted to wait it out in the hotel after having been able to speak to my family. I was not good with driving long distances. I get easily lost, so I did not want to take a chance. I did not feel that it was safe for me to drive while I felt this overwhelming sadness within me for the people that died in the Twin Towers and for the families that they had left behind. I took it so personally because I knew it could have been me in one of those aircrafts. Allowing myself to get glued to the television was not a wise thing to do. I hardly went out of my room. I sequestered myself in, while I flipped the channel to every possible coverage and comment.

Looking back now, I believe that the repeated images of destruction and chaos played over and over before my eyes contributed to the extreme pain I felt within my heart. Even after I was able to get back home, I became obsessed with September 11th news coverage. As I went back to work I constantly talked about it and watched the sad news, which contributed to what amounted to two months of depression. I would break down crying at different times during the day. The pain in my chest from the deep sadness was constant. I had unconsciously allowed myself to be so swept up by the tragedy that it had mentally and physically made me ill. I was not like myself anymore; I felt like I was trapped in someone else's world.

Thank goodness I snapped back to reality. I realized that life has to go on and that I cannot let my emotions overwhelm me so much that I do not enjoy life. I went back into my positive readings of books that taught me about psychology, health, spirituality, and relationships. Now with a better understanding of the ability to let go of emotions that can hurt, I want my readers to understand that you too have the power to let go and turn that corner and feel better about yourself and about the life that you choose to live in.

How about the fear of losing the love and affection of someone dear? This type of fear can be most devastating. It cuts through the heart and ego of a person. So many men and women lose hope in the name of love. Some have died of inability to accept change in love and affection, or the discovery that intimacy they thought they had shared with someone was an illusion.

Love is richer when reciprocated. If the other person has fallen out of love with you, salvation is hard to find. Can you force someone to love you back just because you still have feelings for him or her? A journey on a one-way street is lonely. So no matter how it hurts, no matter that at the moment of truth you have realized that the person you love has lost their feelings for you, gather your strength and let go. Just let it be, because chasing someone who does not want you is like swimming against the current. The energy you spend is wasted. Out of the millions of people out there, surely one day you will find someone new, someone who will one day adore you and accept you for who you are and love you with all your imperfections. Look within yourself: you have so much more love to give. Be patient, love will soon find you.

Have you experienced extreme anger before? Do you remember how terrible you felt when you were in that situation? Anger is a destructive emotion that can disturb your peace. When anger stirs you in a particularly drastic way, it can elevate your blood pressure, which can cause you to get sick. Overwhelming yourself with this negative emotion can unbalance you and make you erupt in violence, causing more aggravating consequences.

In my early thirties, a doctor told me that I had three small fibroids in my uterus but not to worry about it, they needed to be monitored but were usually harmless. I neglected to have it monitored, and several years later another doctor found out that one of the fibroids had gotten very large, as large as a head of a baby. No wonder that no matter how much I worked out my tummy always seem to protrude! My periods became longer, sometimes lasting for two weeks. I became pale and anemic. Flying a 105 hours in the air every month was taking a toll on my body. I found myself unable to breath well at 35,000 feet. My energy level was very low. The doctor advised me to make a quick decision. She said, "I can take the fibroid and keep the uterus intact if you still want to have another child but you have to conceive within the year after the removal; otherwise the fibroid can grow again."

My current husband, Kevin, and I were dating at that time, and he already had two kids, while I had my son, Michael, from my previous marriage. Michael had been begging me to get remarried because he wanted to have a baby brother or sister. Being the only son, he craved company. I explained to my young son the choice in the simplest language he could understand. I also told him that if I married Kevin he would have Kevin's children to play with, a ready-made brother and sister. After a bit of thinking my son said, "It is OK mom, I understand." Kevin did not have the desire to have more kids, and I surely did not feel like going back to those early diaper stages as well. We were both sure that we want to get married and be together. I made up my mind and told my doctor that I wanted her to remove my uterus, since the periods were annoying me so much at that point.

She then explained to me that she had to put me on medication that would shrink the fibroid so that it would make it easier for her to do the operation. She warned me that the medicine could give me temporary symptoms of menopause. I never thought anything about it until after I took the medication. I became a completely a different person, a very angry agitated person. I snapped so easily at anyone. One day my son failed to put away his toys, and I almost tripped on one going up the stairs. Such a small thing made me scream so loud at the top of my voice, until I saw the horrified look on the face of my son. His face became so confused, his eyebrows tilted up, questioning, as he said to me, "Mom what happened to you? Why are you so angry these days?" I felt so bad, tried to compose myself and apologized to my son. I explained to him that I was on a medication that made me this way, and asked him to be patient with me and stay out of my way when I got too unpredictable.

I had to really dig in to work on the controlling the ugly destructive emotion. My hormones were a mess, and I was experiencing temporary hot flashes at a young age. I tried to catch myself before each outburst and say, "This is not me, calm down, calm down." I took deep breaths that helped me regain my composure. Even when it was a challenge, I didn't want to let anger overcome me entirely. The operation was a success, thankfully the medication wore off, my hormones went back to normal and I am back to my old self.

Yes, there are certain situations as well as certain people that can annoy and anger you. Think before you speak. Get your anger under control, no matter how compelled you are to burst into an excessive negative emotional discourse. Do not let your anger overrun you into rage. When someone angers you, you have actually allowed that person to make you feel that way. Losing control can make you lose face. It can be very embarrassing. No matter how righteous your stand may seem, control yourself. It is all up to you to keep your composure and be mature enough to catch yourself and ask, "Is it really worth it?"

Reframe your mind. Take a deep breath. Remember that you have the ability to rule your emotions. Change your mental direction. Allow rationality to emerge. Use thoughtful caring words in a low tone of voice to ease the tension, dissolving anger in its infancy. You can also try doing something different: go for a long vigorous walk or a run in a park. Fresh air can revive you. Take deep breaths and count backward from ten to one. It can relax your senses. You can also take a long relaxing shower: water has a way of distressing your mind and body. Savor the water as it washes away your negative emotions. Make sure to drink a lot of water as well. Soon enough your heartbeat will calm down. You will be able to think rationally again.

Your ability to walk away from a bad situation is a sure sign of maturity. Your self-control and your composure keep you at a higher level. You simply refuse to add fuel to the unpleasant emotion of anger, no matter what the circumstances are at any given moment. Your awareness will give you a true understanding why it pays not to lose control.

Remember that peaceful relationships with people are more important than the problems and conflicts. Conflicts can, in the long run, brew hatred in the heart. Hatred can deteriorate your mind and body. It can create walls of imprisonment for your soul. It brings pain and unhappiness. Deep hatred can cause depression. Depression can cause physical ailments.

Why waste your mind, body and soul? Forgive people who have offended you. We are all human. We all make mistakes. Love even those who may have hurt you. Be a bearer of love, peace, and courage. You are at peace when your mind, body and soul are in total harmony. Peace lives in you because you as a whole are in complete balance. You are able to make meaningful relationships around you, living life as it comes. You are able to control your negative emotions and let them go. Letting go frees up a lot of space for your creative thinking and growth. Rule your emotions as you navigate through life. Uphold the value of each moment, knowing that the power of your choice can make you or break you. Your relationship is more important than any event, circumstance, or conflicts that you and your loved ones are going through.

How to Rule Your Emotions to Achieve Success and Happiness:

1. Acknowledge the freedom of choice.
2. Put your relationships first.

PART 3:

# Creating a Good Foundation

# CHAPTER 13

# Appreciation and Love for Self

What a man thinks of himself, that is which
determines, or rather indicates, his fate.
—*Henry David Thoreau*

## YOU ARE A GIFT

Love yourself. You are unique and special in so many ways.
There is no one like you. Look at yourself in the mirror and
appreciate what you see. Accept the reflection of the work of
art that is you. You are a gift to your family. You are a gift to
nature. You are a gift to all of humanity. You are born with
an innate capacity to develop and enhance what has been
given to you. As you grow, your doubts and fears interfere
with your growth.

Do you remember your fearlessness as a child? The world
was a playground full of wonder.

Growing up in the Philippines, as I did, can make a child
very resourceful when it comes to playtime. I was often
climbing trees with my friends. We would look for a big
branch, climb up, and simply sit there relaxing and enjoying
the breeze. We would take salt with us. Up in a guava tree, we
would pick the fruit and dip it in a bit of salt, which makes for

a great snack on a sunny afternoon. We ate the fruit of the tree while we were up on the branches. For fun when we got bored, we would find a good branch to hang on, a branch that was strong enough to hold our weight. One at a time each one of us hung on to a strong branch with our hands while our bodies were dangling, creating momentum, swinging our bodies back and forth, and then dropping ourselves onto the grassy ground, rolling, screaming, and laughing. Amazingly, we did not break any limbs.

Other times we created caves out of huge leaves. Hanging around my brother Sunny, I watched as he and his friends collected spiders inside matchboxes. We had spider fights. On a long thin stick, usually coming from the palm leaf, one kid puts a spider on one end and another on the opposite end. Two spiders meet in the middle and fight. The spider that stays on the stick becomes the winner. We also played marbles against other kids. We collected marbles of all colors, taking very good care of them so that they stayed spotless without any breakage. I was mystified by the ranging colors of those tiny objects.

When you are young and carefree, the world offers so much promise. I loved it when it rained. When I was a child, our parents allowed us to play outside in the rain with all our friends. It was fun and cool. If one lives in a tropical climate with 90-degree heat, the rain becomes a welcome event, a relief from the heat.

Remember what it feels like to be fearless and full of wonder and excitement like a child. As we grow older, many of our experiences can make us fear what lies ahead. We become too afraid to make a mistake. Let no fear hinder you from what you want in life.

## TAKE CARE OF YOUR MIND, BODY, AND SOUL

When you love yourself, you take better care of your mind, body, and soul. The mind is the engine, the body is the vehicle, and the soul provides the fuel. An engine needs to be in top condition to work its best. Make sure to invest money and time to keep your mind engine sharp. Your body is the shell that carries both mind and soul. A body transforms depending on the investments made in the mind. However, it is the soul that gives the extraordinary human machine its drive.

## CONTINUOUSLY INCREASE YOUR KNOWLEDGE

Enrich your mind with vital information in the area that interests you most. Knowledge can increase your potential for success. You may be lucky to have a good mentor showing you the way.

Life can get so busy that it seems there never is enough time to read. To learn and expand our knowledge, we need to read, listen, or watch something educational. In my early thirties I went through an amazing transformation. After years of neglecting to increase my knowledge, something in me was thirsting for new knowledge. I yearned to start learning again. I was newly divorced and could not afford to buy books. I could hardly afford to take care of my mother and my son. So I decided to get a membership in a nearby library. Then the adventure began. Life seems to expand with every book I read. I read books for personal improvement, books on real estate, autobiographies of successful people, books on psychology, and more. Learning is an endless satisfying quest. I find learning as quenching as the drink of water that gives me life. It is an incredible experience.

Use the information you gather as basis to plan for action. Any information acquired but not used for the purpose of carefully planning the future remains only as potential. There are many highly educated people who live from paycheck to paycheck. To succeed in life, use knowledge to plan for actual action. Take the time to enrich your wisdom by continuously educating yourself. Wisdom is acquired through years of actual application of knowledge and learning from that process. It takes a while to acquire, but once possessed, it enables you to make intelligent decisions. Experience sharpens your ability to find ways to synchronize your knowledge with your intuition.

Intuition is that gut feeling you get about a person or a situation. Be aware of how your body is reacting inside before making major decisions. Learn to align your thoughts with your feelings. Do not ignore your inner physical warnings. Channel your mind to listen to your body in important moments of decisions. Appreciate the signals. It is a way of God communicating to you His messages. Use these signals to guide you.

If something feels right, then by all means go for it in total faith. If it feels wrong, examine the situation closely. You might discover something you had overlooked before. Analyze thoroughly to understand better and plan the best way to go about it.

Intuition is a spiritual faculty and does not
explain, but simply points the way.
—*Florence Scovel Shinn*

## KEEP YOUR BODY FIT

Now let us talk about your body, which houses your soul.
Your body is an awesome mechanism. Love your body. Take
time to exercise. Increased heart rate will give your cells
and organs enough oxygen, making them plump and full
of vitality and energy. Physical activity can increase your
flexibility. It can help your body eliminate toxins.

Exercise can also give you an alert, heightened mental
state: break a sweat to clear your mind. It helps you focus.
It can give you a good feeling of readiness. You are ready
for what lies ahead because you are mentally and physically
alert. Your thought processes seem to flow with ease.

Keeping fit is more of a mental discipline than a physical
one. Once the mind is committed to the task, the body
follows its lead. As a teenager I used to run one hour at dawn
almost every day. I would wake up at four in the morning to
run with a few friends. We chose to do our exercises early
while it was still cool. When the sun was up it could often be
as hot as 85 to 100 degrees. It was awesome to get it done
early before the day started. I was sixteen years old, going
to college while running a full time business in our basement
apartment. As soon as I got home from my workout, I would
prepare the assignments for all of my dressmakers, eat a
quick breakfast, check my assignments, and maybe do a quick

review for an upcoming test. It was a pretty hectic lifestyle, but the exercise grounded me.

To this day I enjoy my workout. I have tried to stay as active as I could throughout the years. There were times when I slacked off and didn't work out for weeks or sometimes a few months. Inches and pounds would start to creep in, but then I would shake myself back into fitness mode. As soon as I started working out again, I started feeling better about myself. My energy was high and I felt more confident. Nutrition and exercise must become a part of the active lifestyle to promote health and longevity.

To achieve these benefits, get up early, and find time to exercise before starting your day. A strong commitment to stay fit will change your attitude toward working out. You will start enjoying the physical activities because you feel so good inside. You will face life with a healthy, invigorating, ageless energy that is derived from your intelligent choices. Living healthy will reward you with a great quality of life.

## THE QUALITY OF YOUR LIFE INVIGORATES YOU

Improving your quality of life can lengthen your days on earth. Being aware of this can help you properly direct your actions toward health and a satisfying life.

Good nutrition is one part of this. When you know the basic functions of food and how much your body needs to perform effectively, you will become conscious of what you put into your mouth. Read about nutrition so you can carefully eliminate unhealthy processed food from your diet. Choose nutritious food that can help you gain energy instead of unwanted weight. This kind of knowledge can give you increased awareness of how your diet is affecting your life. Such awareness enhances the quality of your food intake.

Eating more nutritious food will start making you feel better and younger, increasing your confidence. Having more confidence will transform you. What is in you can manifest in your environment. When you take care of your body, a more wholesome inner self can emerge. You feel good when your body is fit. Your clothes look better on you. You can look at the mirror and take pride in finding a total package of health and beauty before you.

> What lies behind us and what lies before
> us are tiny matters compared to what lies
> within us.
>
> —*Ralph Waldo Emerson*

## NOURISH YOUR SOUL

Inside the package of your body, is your soul. An active life force sits within you, giving you the zest for life. You are an eternal being that existed even before the formulation of your physical composition. Your soul is in you for the purposes of loving, growing, and learning. The lessons you learn in this life will take your soul closer to the Higher Being.

Love yourself completely, mind, body, and soul. The power of love is strong. It can give you upbeat confidence. You can only give that which you have: when you love yourself, you can love others. Make yourself full of love so it overflows. The love that you give out comes back to you a thousandfold.

I believe in spending some time each day staying in touch with my inner being. I do this usually at night. You can choose any time of the day that best works for you. I reflect on the life that I have, grateful for just being here. Quiet moments of meditation can recapture my inner peace after a busy day, giving me a sense of balance. I pray for my family and all the people on earth to find love, peace, and happiness. This is my goal in life, to help others find fulfillment. I want to help other people smile again.

## PEACE AND HARMONY WITHIN

Peace and harmony can be found in a content soul that lives for each moment. The tranquil soul is rich. It is in the quiet stillness of the moment that answers are discovered. Delve into an inner sanctuary of complete calm from within that you may function wholly. Experience inner healing in the midst of calm. Be at peace with yourself. Accept what you are and who you are with all your glory and limitations. Your imperfections makes you unique. Your excellence in the talents that you have well cultivated through the years overcomes your limitations in other areas.

Accepting yourself is equal to loving yourself. Love for self creates harmony between your inner world and outer world. Without love for yourself, it will be very hard to love another human being. You can only end up in chaotic relationships. Lack of love for oneself brews excessive insecurity. Insecurity makes you live in constant lack, like nothing in the world can ever make you feel happy and complete.

Find peace by finding time to be alone with yourself. You can go for long walks, run, or ride a bike, or you may prefer to meditate, read, or knit. Do whatever brings you solace, whatever makes you feel more relaxed. Learning to find time to reach your inner quiet self helps you face your outer life with fresh enthusiasm. It gives you a new surge of energy.

Remember that our true self resides within our physical make up. Our essence within can be described as complete, perfect, unlimited, powerful, and eternal. Our body is a temple, a temporary manifestation in which the soul resides. It is like the cover of a book. The soul is the true self, the content of the book. Our body is the cover, the clothing of the soul. Therefore, what is important is that we bring our awareness to the fullness of the power within us. Know that you have what it takes to do incredible things. Seek wisdom, that you may find it. Once wisdom is acquired, your insecurities will start to fade.

Wisdom expands confidence. Confidence builds up your power to achieve more things of greater importance. Peace transforms you with gentle grace, making your life more desirable to live in. Life changes like the waves that dance in the ocean. Ride the waves with gentle peace to find happiness.

To Appreciate and Love Yourself, You Need to Take Care of Your:

Mind
Body
Soul

On the worksheets on the following pages, write down five things each that you will do to take care of your mind, your body, and your soul. Write your words in the present tense. This injects the steps in your life as though you are already doing them. Making them a part of your reality now. It is more effective to condition your mind to the eventual fulfillment of this contract that you make to yourself, than to always speak in the future tense, as if the fulfillment is remote and not yet real. Writing is the key to make your dreams happen. When you write down what you will do, you become committed to what you have promised yourself.

Sample List of Ways to Take Care of Yourself:
- I meditate 20 minutes a day.
- I work out one hour each day.
- I listen to educational audio books while I drive in my car and while I work out.
- I entertain positive thoughts to enrich my mind.
- I visualize my goals vividly, feeling the emotions of achievement.

Write down five steps that you can do to take care of your mind:

1._____

2._____

3._____

4._____

5._____

Write down five steps that you can do to take care of your body:

1._____

2._____

3._____

4._____

5._____

Write down five steps that you can do to take care of your soul:

1._____

2._____

3._____

4._____

5._____

CHAPTER 14

❦

## Heal the Mind, Heal the Body

Body and mind, like man and wife, do not
always agree to die together.
—*Charles Caleb Colton*

Keep your mind strong. A strong mind creates a strong body. Your body follows the command of your inner voice, so think in terms of abundance of health. Mental clarity increases physical vitality. Let your mind rule every cell in your body by allowing only positive mental visions of utmost active physical health. The mind rules the body. A strong mind can alter the physiology of the body. Healing can start from the will of wanting to be whole again.

Let me relate to you a story about my mother's sister, my Aunt Maming. One day she came over to our house after visiting the doctor's office. She told us that her x-rays showed several stones in her kidney. She was very sad and worried because the doctor told her that she needed to be operated on. The doctor picked a date for her operation. She asked my mother to pray for her and to take her to the church to be prayed over by the charismatic members. My mother was a dedicated member of a church that had a healing ministry. Members laid their hands over the sick as a group as they prayed fervently for healing. The two sisters went to church and my aunt was prayed over by many members of the church. Then aunt Maming went home to Carmen, Cebu. Many days later she came by the house again and informed my mother that it was the day that the doctor had appointed for her operation. Aunt Maming said that she urged the doctor to take one more x-ray before the operation. When the doctor examined the new x-rays he was confused; he could not locate the stones. He took the old x-ray and placed it next to the new x-ray, and it was clear that the stones were gone. He simply could not explain what had happened. Aunt Maming happily told the doctor that her prayers had been answered. She proceeded to tell the doctor about being prayed over at her sister's church. The doctor shrugged his shoulders and said, "Well, it looks like a miracle happened for you. Go and celebrate. I don't know what to say." We were so happy that Aunt Maming did not have to go through the operation. What a wonderful blessing.

Is it the combined positive energy of the people praying for the sick that helps them? Is it the boost of faith of the one being prayed for that opens them up to healing? Many experiments have been made that have promising data. People who have been prayed for tend to heal faster. Hopefully a day will come when science will have a way to measure the effect of prayers.

When a person stresses over things, it puts a toll on the body. When a person get stressed out, the brain releases the stress hormone cortisol, causing increased blood pressure and increased blood sugar. Cortisol has an immune-suppressive action. It can slow down the body's disease-fighting response. People who are frequently too stressed out gain weight around their midsection. Stress will not make you feel good and it will not make you look good either. Avoid becoming too preoccupied by stress. Use your mind to enhance your health with the positive thoughts that you cultivate.

To use the power of the mind to heal the body, it is essential that the person wants to get better. That choice will jumpstart the healing process. Illness is the breaking down of the perfect rhythmic mechanism of the awesome physical body created for you to use to enjoy life. The quality of your thoughts has a direct relationship to the quality of your health and your life. Choosing quality thoughts provides a constant fuel of energy throughout your body to maintain health.

On the other hand, since the mind dictates to the body, internalizing the fear of becoming sick can make you sick. Symptoms of what had been an imaginary illness will start materializing. It becomes a self-fulfilling prophecy. Fear of ill health finds a way to come to life when it is constantly invited to occupy your mind.

Invite great health instead; visualize your body in top physical health. Keep a peaceful mental clarity. Imagine working out everyday. Vividly see the fit body you want, admiring the athletic legs and strong arms. Feel the emotions of owning that body. Hold these images in your mind as often as you can throughout the day.

Mental conditioning will increase your enthusiasm for keeping your body fit. You will look forward to eating healthy. As you become more aware and careful with your food intake, feel full quicker. Working out becomes so much more joyable when you know it is good for you. So you start working out daily. Endorphins are released from the brain after each good work out, increasing that good feeling inside. Physical transformations occur when your desire is reinforced by the clear visual imagery of the fit body that you want.

Change your body by replacing fearful images of illness with positive visual images of the fit, strong, healthy mind and body that you want. By changing the vision, you can alter matter to that which you desire.

## STRESS CAN MAKE THE BODY ILL

Allowing events, circumstances, and people to stress you can undermine your health. Stress is self-inflicted. No one, nothing can make you stressed out but yourself. Life will have its ups and downs. Your attitude toward the events and people in your life is important in maintaining outstanding physical health. How you respond is your choice. Knowing that you have a choice that allows you to control your health and destiny can be the beginning of your own awakening.

It starts in your mind. Choose positive loving thoughts as you walk your journey in life. Take good care of your body through proper nutrition and daily exercise. Eating healthy can boost your immune system, preventing you from getting sick. Daily exercise can keep your body flexible and toned.

When a person chooses to fill the mind with negativities, disappointments, and hatred, the power house deteriorates, becoming dysfunctional. A malfunction of the power source diminishes the transfer of energy to the body. As the mind is weakened, the person becomes susceptible to diseases of the physical body due to the low production of disease fighting antibodies. With a weak immune system, the body easily becomes an open target for viruses and other diseases.

## MIND, FEAR, AND THE BODY

Fear is the child of your imagination. It cannot exist if you do not allow it to. Fear materializes when allowed to pollute and manipulate the mind. Your mind influences your physical functions. A mind bombarded by too much fear destroys the functions of the body. There is a certain dance that happens between the mind and the body. A stressed-out, overly aggravated mind can disorient physical cells, making them fall ill. Do not allow fears to overwhelm you. They are imaginary things that are not proven true. Build up your confidence to face life bravely.

## THE MIND NEEDS REST

How much time do you sleep at night? Each individual has a unique sleep need. Be sure to get enough sleep at night to rejuvenate your body. Try to plan to get the amount of sleep you need, however long you need to feel fresh. A good night's rest can make you feel good for the new day. When you feel awesome, you feel ready for the challenges of the day.

Lack of sleep can make you feel tired even as you get up. Some people start a day with a headache. How can you be effective when you do not feel good at the onset of the day? Give yourself ample rest so you can wake up full of energy.

How much time do you spend to play and relax? Do you

have time for your family? Spend time to play with your loved ones. Go on vacation with your family. Leave the interuptions of modern technology behind. Quality playtime can recharge your batteries.

## RELEASE NEGATIVE EMOTIONS

It is important not to harbor hatred for anyone. Hatred can hurt you physically and mentally. It slows down the fluidity of your inner mechanism. What is within you finds a way to manifest into your reality. Guard your thoughts and your inner desires so they retain the essence of goodness toward mankind, nature, and most especially for yourself. Positive thoughts can give you a pleasing disposition, your inner self to become peaceful, your relationships to be enhanced, and your health to prosper.

## AGING GRACEFULLY

Physical organisms have various transitions throughout their lives. Life as we perceive it in the human physical form starts upon conception of the fetus within the mother. The birth of a child is a wonderful, glorious moment. A child is a gift from the universe. Within each child is a soul, infinite from the main source. An everlasting energy that carries each human being throughout their earthly life and beyond.

The soul is born for a reason. Each human being is here for a purpose. It is up to you to delve within and find your primary purpose in life. Navigate life with awareness, go with the flow of constant changes, and then learn from the challenges. Allow the soul to learn, love, and grow. As time goes by, the physical form undergoes many changes. Depending on how well you take care of your mind and body, you can stay healthy and active through your later years. Time is an earthly aspect, however, eternity knows no time and space. The soul stays young forever. It is as fresh as the day it was conceived in its mother's womb.

Do you worry about growing old? Some worry about getting old, thinking about the physical limitations and sexual limitations and dwindling mental capacity. But worrying about growing old will not make you any younger. Growing old is an inescapable part of life. If you view it in a positive light, growing old has a lot of advantage to it. You would have acquired enough wisdom to conquer the challenges of life, increasing your self-confidence.

Grow old gracefully. Do not waste your time worrying about the passage of time. Take pride in the life you have lived, and the quality of all the experiences of your past. Enjoy the process but do live for the present. Fill your awareness with enthusiasm for life. Take great care of your mind by daily reading, solving word puzzles, and writing into your diary twice a day. Most importantly, think positive! Start a good exercise regimen and commit to it. Your energy will soar, and you will feel absolutely fantastic no matter how old you are. Age is just a number, and the body is just a temporary clothing of the soul. Now just live for the moment, savor the pleasure that life offers you.

## MYSTERY OF DEATH

Birth is celebrated, while death is mourned. But like birth, death is a part of life. It is common knowledge that all of us will experience death. It is an inescapable reality. When the time will come, everyone will have to go through it.

Do you know that for every cell that dies in the body, many more new cells are formed to take its place? Throughout the human lifetime, physical cells have died many deaths and have been replaced by the birth of millions of other cells. Think of death as nothing but a change of phase, a transitional stage of rebirth. Death is not the end. Death is the transition from the physical existence to the spiritual existence. Matter is dissolved back into the earth where it belongs as the spirit is lifted up to go back into the light of everlasting life. Back to a life where there is no room for pain, a life bounded only by beauty, wisdom, and love. It is the beginning of life, where time and space do not exist.

Living life fully without fear will lengthen the life that you have. Death is a homecoming that deserves a celebration in heaven.

# CHAPTER 15

## *What Is Faith?*

1. Faith is a total surrender in the abundant goodness of the universe. Ralph Waldo Emerson wrote, "All that Adam had, all that Caesar could, you have and can do....Go, therefore, and build your own world." There is enormous potential that awaits each human being. Recognize the resources at hand. Cultivate creativity in using the resources that you find to develop your potential. All people have equal opportunities, except most of us missed noticing the many doors awaiting to be opened.

2. Faith is the knowledge that a positive force dwells within us. There is unlimited guidance from the Higher Being. Learn to ask for what you want in prayer or meditation. You will eventually hear the voice in your head guiding you with each decision that you make. You are never alone. Faith is a recognition of the complete potential that we need to tap into to reach success. Believe that you have what it takes to create the life that you want. Focus on your ability to expand your world. The world is an open market, free for all to partake in. There is not much difference between a regular person and Bill Gates. Bill Gates's success is due to his ability to recognize the great potential of an idea. He then went to work with utmost faith and passion to pursue what he deeply believed in. Gates and his partner Paul Allen created

Microsoft, a billion-dollar business. He has now retired to focus on his philanthropy work with the Bill and Melinda Gates Foundation.

3. Faith is the intense belief within us that all things are possible as much as the degree that we want it. If you want something, want it with all that you have. The feeling must come from the heart. A want that you just have to have must take root in your gut. There is no other way but for the universe to grant exactly what it is that you want. This is how faith works. It works because you know it has to happen even if at some point you may not know how. What matters is that you have accepted within you that it will happen.

My mother spends at least three to four hours in prayer every single day. Praying is what she loves to do now that she is older. Her prayers are powerful. Many relatives and friends call on my mother asking for her prayers, whether it is about health, work, or relationship matters. Her friends and relatives have a habit of giving her a list of details of what to pray for. Even my husband asks her to pray for his business contracts to go through. I tell my friends that my mother is within earshot of God. God grants her prayers because she prays so long that God just wants to give her what she wants to shut her up. She is the sweetest thing in the world.

# CHAPTER 16

# Marriage and Partnerships

A promise of a lifetime together is a serious thing. To withstand the tests and challenges of time, a union of two people who want to grow old together hand in hand need a strong commitment. Therefore, each individual must understand the gravity of the responsibility that comes within the union.

When it comes to relationships, I believe that experience is a good teacher. A friend of mine named Eddie met Janice in college. They dated for a few years before finally getting married. Looking back, Eddie remembered how they bickered about the smallest things while they were still dating. Later on, the added pressure of raising a family of three kids escalated the disagreements further. There were rampant fights about money and responsibilities. While Eddie worked long hours to provide for the family, Janice expected Eddie to relieve her of taking care of the kids as soon as he got home from work. Eddie was very careful when it came to finances, while Janice loved expensive things. Eddie thought it was not necessary to indulge in certain luxuries while their three kids were young and there was only one household income. After 15 years they decided to get divorced. Divorce is never easy especially when children are involved. Change was necessary in a situation where both husband and wife were constantly fighting and could not find common ground. A few years later Janice is happily remarried. Eddie was very sad after the divorce but eventually settled down and got married to someone who better complements him.

Relationships can be very rewarding. It takes a lot of compromise, and exercise in patience. The process gets better with maturity.

Still, the decision to marry must be weighed carefully. Ask yourself the following questions: Can I live with this person for the rest of my life? Am I willing to compromise to make the relationship work? Can I accept the individuality of the other person and respect his or her views? There are countless questions one must ponder before embarking on such a lifetime decision. Make sure to make your decision wisely if you are about to leap into a marriage or a serious partnership.

If you are still single seeking to find a suitable partner in life, look for a mate who is positive, happy, and supportive and who shares similar interests and outlook on life with you. Constant bickering about small matters in the beginning of a relationship is a signal for even greater trouble in the future. Do not expect the other person to change. You have to accept the other person as you have found him or her and live with your choice. People need to change for themselves, not for your satisfaction. Decisions to change must come from within. If you see that you would need the person to change for you to be happy, let the person go while still at the dating stages and avoid spending much emotional pain and money in future divorce proceedings. Everything in life involves risks, but the better you calculate your risk, the better your decisions are.

If you are already in a marriage, use 101 percent of what you've got to make the marriage a happy, fulfilling one. Give your utmost love and compassion. Be there for your loved one as you navigate life together.

Express your love openly and sincerely. When hugging, do hug warmly with a sincere thought of positive connection. When kissing your lover or partner, kiss with passion. Let go of ill thoughts and ill feelings before going to bed. Keep the bedroom as a sacred place of peace for you and your loved one. Taking the problems of the day within the confines of the bedroom can ruin your relationship. Think of the great qualities of your loved one no matter how the rest of the day went. Feel gratitude for being able to share this special time with the one you love.

If you want your spouse or partner to treat you better, treat him or her in a special way first. If after you treat this person extra special, he or she still treats you badly, treat him or her with double the compassion, all you can muster. After giving all the love and compassion you can as many times as this person has treated you badly, then either you will have finally turned this individual completely around and be enjoying a great relationship with love or this person will have chosen to continue with the negative treatment toward you, in which case, it may be hopeless. If that's so, the best thing to do is to reevaluate your relationship. You may be better off being alone than to live in a constant battle. Choose to be with someone who is open to experiencing compassionate existence.

If you are unhappy in your marriage, seek counseling

and find ways of saving it. It is worth the maximum effort, especially when children are involved. Compromise and forgive. Use compassion to mend your relationship. If you are at fault, accept responsibility for your mistakes and ask for forgiveness. Take in your pride; the good of the family is most important.

However, if after you have gone to counseling and given a 101 percent of what you've got to keep it together, you are still unhappy, assess if this is a relationship that you want to be in for the rest of your life. Life is too short to live unhappily with someone you are not compatible with. Life is full of changes: people change, situations change. If two people can grow together hand in hand, giving each other support, the relationship gains strength as love grows and bond people tighter. But if two people disagree to the extent of having rampant fights, love dies along the path. If partners are unable to see eye to eye, the bond is broken.

Marriage or a partnership is wonderful if it is born with total commitment, selflessness, love, and compassion.

## LOVE AND JEALOUSY

Jealousy takes away the glory of the actual moment you are currently spending with the person you love. To love and be loved is an inexplicable magical thing that no words ever written can fully capture. Intense electrical magnetic attraction that binds two hearts is the ultimate expression of paradise on earth. A lot of jealousy is unfounded, the causes imagined. Trust your loved one. Appreciate what great love you share. To love is to trust; if trust is lost, the home crumbles into pieces. Commit to give a 100 percent of what you have in your relationship. Why change your heaven? Be here in the now, flow with the rhythmic current of pulsating love. Bathe in the light of its glory.

# CHAPTER 17

## Harmony at Home

If we have no peace, it is because we have
forgotten that we belong to each other.
—*Mother Theresa*

Your home should be a safe, comfortable haven for your family. The warmth of your dwelling and the love shared within has a therapeutic effect. It reenergizes and invigorates the spirit each day. A harmonious home is vital to your success. Happiness at home as well as in your personal life overflows to happiness at work. When you are not happy at home, you lose your focus. Focus is necessary in reaching your goal. A distracted mind becomes blurry, making the future uncertain. You need a clear mind to see your vision of success. Peace elevates your concentration, making your goals more defined. Harmony at home is therefore vital in order to achieve great success.

### THE IMPORTANCE OF FAMILY

Family is a treasure: put your loved ones first in your heart. They are the reason why you work. You work hard because you want to take care of yourself and your family. You want to improve your situation in life and your career so that you can provide a comfortable life for the people you love.

## USE YOUR TIME EFFECTIVELY

Plan to work effectively during the hours that you are supposed to be working so that you will not end up bringing work home. You want to be able to use quality time when you are home to truly engage and connect with your loved ones. Show your undivided love and attention when you are with them. Your family is the pillar that holds you up and keeps you in great spirits. Give them the love and care that they need. Be there fully for them in mind and body.

Remember that you get what you give, so give generously of your time to your loved ones and friends who are close to your heart. Your family and your close relationships come first. Your strong relationships can give you great leverage to succeed. Having a good support system gives you peace of mind. Peace of mind allows the uninterrupted flow of creative thoughts. Your good state of mind and well-being increases the quality and productivity of your work, increasing your self-confidence as well as your income.

## AWARENESS OF SHARED
## FINANCIAL RESPONSIBILITY

Let your family know their contribution to the financial responsibility of your household. Sit down with them once a month when preparing the bills to be sent out. This practice will make the children understand that money does not just grow on trees, making them become more responsible. Let them understand the value of each dollar, that they may become aware of the expenses involved in running a household. Encourage each family member to be thrifty.

Turn the lights off when no one is in the room, turning the television off when no one is watching, and turn the faucet tight so the water doesn't drip. Discuss the importance of refraining from buying anything that is not of vital use. Your family will not demand from you extravagant things of wasteful nature when they have a better, deeper view of how much money is involved in providing for everyone's needs. When everyone is involved in the financial planning, there will be fewer quarrels about money. A lot of marriages break up due to financial issues and misunderstandings. Address these issues from the beginning to keep the family at peace.

Good relationships multiply the positive vibrations in your daily life, making your goals easier to define. Compatibility of vision for the future between you and your loved ones is power. Respect individuality and encourage human uniqueness. Then appreciate the differences among you, striking a balance within the family between shared visions and individual goals.

Conflict within the family breaks the fluidity of thought, decreasing energy among all members. It is a barrier to success. Make your family a priority. You work in order to take good care of the needs of your family. A lot of people work so hard that they spend very little time with their family. Relations become strained and communication disintegrates, leaving everyone feeling lost. Instead, keep your loved ones as number one in your heart. Your family can provide you with inspiring energy for success. Remember the purpose of your work is to take care of your family.

Seek to work effectively in less time to have more free time to be with your family. Get organized. Plan in the evening, what you want to do the next day. Plan on Sundays what your activities and responsibilities will be for the week. Make sure to include time for your loved ones. Your efforts will reward you with peace. Peace and harmony at home opens up the road to creativity. From creativity you can embark toward an array of possibilities, which if acted upon can bring you success. Success can give you and your family comfort. Your extra resources will be a chance for you to share your graces to those who have less than what you have.

## SPEND TIME WITH YOUR LOVED ONES

During the weekends, spend time with people who are important to you. Spend time with your family and friends. Spend these precious moments with people you care for without the distractions of cell phone and computer. Your loved ones deserve your full attention. Focus this time on reconnecting. Completely give of yourself. Learn to just relax. Soak yourself with love for the people who truly matter to you.

In the evenings when you get home, unwind with soothing music instead of turning on the television. Negative news and shows can give you more stress. Spend time with your loved ones. This will be a good time to see how everyone's day went. If you have children, please be patient with them. Keep a low, loving tone of voice when speaking with your loved ones. Do not take the stress from work to your home. It can be toxic to your home life.

## SEEK TO UNDERSTAND YOUR
## FAMILY BY LISTENING

Turn off the television when eating dinner with your family, and your conversations will become more meaningful, enhancing your connectedness. Good communication is important for keeping a peaceful atmosphere at home. Listen intently to understand the needs of your family. Listening can give you deeper understanding, and along with understanding comes compassion for your loved ones. Compassion for one another can give the family peace. Experiencing peace is magical in bringing out your creative faculties, which you need to be truly successful in life.

## PEACE INCREASES YOUR FOCUS

Peace helps you achieve success by freeing up energy that could have been tangled in chaos. Peace helps you focus, giving you clarity of thought and mental vision. Your focus allows you to see clearly the direction you are heading. When you know where you are going, you are more likely to arrive at your destination. Without direction, you tend to travel aimlessly through a maze, not finding your way.

Peace is a gift you owe to yourself. Search for peace. Choose to be peaceful. Do not let technology over run your life with endless noisy distractions. Give all that you can to enrich your relationships. Exercise patient determination while giving your best at home and at work. Harmony at home is a foundation for your successful future. Happiness overflows into success in business and career.

Why is Harmony at Home Important for Success?

Harmony at home and your personal life can increase your focus and sense of well-being, as well as provide a stable support system.

# CHAPTER 18

## *Learning Begins at Home*

Children imitate what they observe and experience from a tender age. Parents who are nurturing, loving, and encouraging raise children who are confident, courageous, and ambitious.

In my case, growing up with an alcoholic father was very difficult. However, the love of my nurturing mother neutralized the devastating effects that it could have done to my young mind. The separation of my parents was traumatic, as my father took me away from the hospital when I was taking care of my bedridden mother after a serious bus accident. I was confused and yet I strove to be strong. I had to grow up too quickly at the age of nine.

My father took my brother and me to Manila. We lived with different relatives and friends. Father and Sunny could not see eye to eye. Eventually my brother left for Cebu City to live with my Uncle Bebeng, a brother of my father.

Meanwhile, my father rented a room for me. I had to live with two older ladies. They were sisters that had never gotten married. Luckily they treated me well. My father lived somewhere else and just visited me every now and then. I felt lost. I was so young without my mother and living with ladies I barely knew. My grades plummetted. I could not focus. I stared into space, dazed, teachers did not know what to make of me.

However, that separation was the beginning of a change. When my mother got out of the hospital, she investigated where we were, found us, and then we started a new life without my father. Then peace and happiness was what we experienced daily even in the midst of very trying times. My strong, positive mother instilled within us strength of character, hope for the best, and the will to survive.

Many parents who have addiction problems and are abusive have raised children who at some point in their adult life struggle with emotional pain, some resorting to the use of drugs and alcohol. Not all children of alcoholic and abusive parents turn out this way. Some children at a tender age develop strength to survive. A sense of separating themselves from the pain of growing up makes them stay away from anything addictive and abusive. In some instances, these children looked to someone outside their home for guidance and approval. A caring, thoughtful teacher can have a big positive impact. In other instances, it is a relative or a neighbor who finds time to show some love to these neglected children.

A good example of rising above from a very abusive past is the story of Kevin Lewis, author of *The Kid*. Kevin grew up in South London. His father was an alcoholic and his mother a very rough unfit mother. Kevin suffered from constant hunger and brutal beatings from both parents. Kids in school bullied him and his siblings because they were different. They went to school in very old dirty clothes, they hardly ever showered, and they all smelled bad. Their mother never cleaned the house. The children went to school without breakfast, and had to resort to stealing food from the meal boxes of their classmates or going through the garbage at school for leftover food to eat.

When Kevin got a little bigger he would wake up early in the morning, around five o'clock, to find the milk man so he could help deliver milk to make some money to buy food for himself and his siblings. On weekends he would take a bucket and a sponge and knock on doors to offer his services to wash cars for people. On one occasion he was almost molested by one of his customer who liked young boys. Kevin got away and never went back to that home, but he did not let that incident stop him from working.

Eventually he escaped from the violence at home and was placed in foster care. It was hard for him to be moving from one place to another, but it was better than being hungry and getting beatings from his parents. After experiencing the real world, he dreamed of having a normal life and coming to America, where, in the movies that he saw as a child on television, there seem to be so much freedom.

Kevin had a great connection with one of his foster parents, Allen. Allen taught Kevin a lot about life and business. It was truly like a father-and-son relationship. Allen became Kevin's mentor, teaching him about life and business. Kevin dreamed about becoming financially well-off one day. But at the age of seventeen, out of foster care and on his own, he was unable to make a proper living and got caught up in the criminal underworld of London. At some point in this chaotic existence, he tried to kill himself by overdosing on pills. Luckily he instead fell into a deep long sleep, and when he awoke, he somehow had gotten the rest his body needed and his mind cleared up.

Kevin turned himself around, making his dream of financial independence alive in his mind again. He was good at sales and making deals, and this time he did it the legal way. Kevin went on to build his own company, and made a lot of money. Some business partners tried to cheat him of his money, but Kevin was determined to stay clean and stay on the right side of the law. He eventually sold part of his business. He is now happily married and is a father of two children.

He wrote the book *The Kid* about his life story and has since written more books. Kevin Lewis was a victim that refused to stay a victim, willing himself to be free of his past demons. He rarely thinks of the past. He instead plans for the future ahead. He dreamed of becoming a stockbroker in America one day.

Reflecting upon the life of Kevin Lewis reminds me of my own childhood. My father was an alcoholic, though on the very rare occasions when he was sober he was the most loving affectionate person. Excessive alcohol changes the personality of the person. My brother and I were very lucky to have the most wonderful mother to raise us after the separation. As a child, I dreamed of a future that was peaceful and unlike what I was experiencing. To this day I cherish my peace. I live to love and promote happiness to all mankind.

Some children of abusive family resort to reading, finding heroes in the characters of inspiring books. Adventures found in the stories become an escape world full of limitless possibilities, shifting children's imagination into a world more desirable than what they are experiencing in the moment and waking up their senses to something they want to have, a life of normalcy and fun. The library becomes a haven of fantasy that a young person trapped in an unhealthy home visits to get away from the chaos.

## THE JOY OF HEALTHY PARENTING

No one can truly comprehend the happiness of becoming a parent until they experience it themselves. Nine months and ten days of eagerly waiting for my son Michael to be born did not prepare me enough for the enormous love I felt when I finally set my eyes on him and held him in my arms. My heart exploded with love.

> There's nothing that can help you
> understand your beliefs more than trying to
> explain them to an inquisitive child.
> —*Frank A. Clark*

Becoming a parent is a growing, selfless experience. It is the crowning glory of human existence. The intense joy is inexplicable; it can open a sleeping heart to a sweet, pure love, beyond compare. Being a parent is an incredible, exciting experience. Each challenge encountered in raising your child strengthens your bond, providing a better hope for tomorrow. Our children hold the future of the world. Show them the value of living with awareness. Show them, that now is what really matters. Their future is embedded in the present moment. Understanding this will enlighten them and allow them to tap into the unlimited creative power from within to enjoy life as it comes, a moment at a time.

Teach your children through your actions. Words can be fleeting when teenagers have a strong tendency to rebel, but the examples that your actions convey can remain in their memory for a long time. Bring your children up with wisdom; show them the way. Hold their hand when they are young that they may not stumble. Engrave hope within their soul by showing them your strength even in the midst of adversities. Raise them with love, respect, and discipline.

Children need nurturing encouragement from their surroundings. It helps to build their wings of courage to achieve their best and pursue making their dreams come true. Give them the glitter of hope to conquer their fears. Then light the path of their dreams to allow them to grow and develop their talents that the world may become a better place.

As an adult, who do you look up to? Is there one special person that you believe has influenced you in the most positive way? What qualities in this person do you admire most? Are there habits that this person possess that you have emulated through the years? No matter what type of home environment you have experienced in your early years, as an adult searching for success and happiness, you can pick the hero you choose to look up to. Learn from your experiences and the experiences from the history of your particular hero. Learn about all the obstacles they have overcome and achievements they have accomplished. If the person who inspires you is the one who mentors you, ask a lot of questions, be like a sponge. Write notes as you capture valuable priceless lessons to apply into your life.

Experiences from a good home:
- Selflessness
- Compassion
- Love
- Nurturing
- Learning
- Growing

# PART 4:

# Attitudes
# for Success

# CHAPTER 19

## Do You Worry Too Much?

What is it that you worry about most? Why do you worry so much about this matter? Do you believe that spending a lot of time worrying will improve your situation? Are you able to think clearly?

When excessive thinking about what you fear most occupies your mind it keeps other things out, hindering you from progress. Worrying intensifies the problem at hand. Imaginary disruptive thinking have temporarily possessed your mind, freezing its ability to take realistic, planned, organized action. Occupation of your mind by this negative entity halts creativity, blocks the creative energy that is needed for any kind of positive outcome. Nothing can be gained from allowing your worries and fears to take hold of your mind. Creativity happens only when positive energy dominates the mind.

You have a choice, if you choose to worry and allow the complexities of the problem to take root in your subconscious mind, your fears will eventually materialize for you. Or you can choose to recognize that the fear or problem is there and then let it go to free yourself some space for creative positive energy to work on creating solutions. Letting go opens up some mental space for the positive energy to come in, awakening up a new awareness that can help tap into great ideas and plans to improve your situation in life.

## ARE YOU CONCERNED ABOUT
## WHAT PEOPLE THINK AND SAY?

Do you feel affected by what people think and say about you? Are you always worried about what they think of you? Are you finding yourself reluctant to act because of what other people may say about your actions? Do not be easily distracted about what others think and say about you. Everybody is entitled to an opinion. An opinion is just an opinion, it does not change who you are. You are a strong entity who can withstand mere opinions.

Unfounded criticism is something you need to ignore or tolerate. Use constructive criticism to your advantage to guide you in improving yourself in areas that you need to work on. You create your own image by how you feel about yourself inside. Walk your path in life with confidence. Others' opinions are the least of your worries. Conduct yourself with respect and empathy for others. Your actions will speak for themselves. Words are like whispers compared to responsible, actual actions.

Groom yourself well, wear appropriate clothes that suit your style, and then all you need to add to your package is confidence and a smile. Be comfortable with who you are, feel good, and be confident with the way you carry yourself. You are the one who will face the world, not anyone else. So please do not waste your time worrying about what people think and say about you.

Excessive worrying can harm you. Realize that you can stop this pattern of thinking. You can take responsibility for your very own thought process. You are in control of your own mind no matter what type of environment you navigate. It is up to you to decide what you want to put into it. If you are seeking to improve your life and enrich it with abundance and fun, you need to eliminate your fears and worries.

## ARE YOU FEELING OVERWHELMED?

Modern society has created many stressed-out people in the process. Technology is overwhelming our senses. Why? It's because we have allowed ourselves to be drowned into the process. Life is so fast paced that there never is enough time to do the things that a person wants to get done. A lot of people resort to drinking a lot of caffeine throughout the day to get jolts of energy. Stress drives other people to find solace in alcohol, feeling that it can relieve their state of disarray. Fast food is a booming industry; nobody seems to have enough time to cook a fresh meal from scratch anymore. The results of this are apparent with the increase of obesity and heart disease in our society.

Pause for a moment and learn to use your time effectively. Use technology to your advantage, but do not let it enslave your attention. Use one hour each day as a sacred time that you spend with yourself to relax your mind and body. A time just for you to regain your sanity, reenergize, and gain peace. You can use this time to meditate, read, or exercise. Make sure to find peace in this special time you spend with yourself. When you have a tranquil soul, you find happiness. Happiness gives you energy to accomplish more within the twenty-four hours that you have. Good moods can help you get more organized than worrying how to get things done.

Feeling good makes you more productive, getting things done with ease. A positive mental attitude will increase your energy for life; you may not need as much caffeine when you can be naturally elevated by your thoughts.

Worries originate from fears, and worrying excessively elevates your stress level. Discipline your mind to dwell instead on thoughts that can build your confidence. Release your fears through the proper use of your mind. Recognize problems, and then let the fear go so that you create some space to invite positive solutions to replace it. Creativity springs out from a mind free of fears. The more you worry and despair, the harder it is to find a way out of the problem. Release the congestion of worry and remind yourself that there is a solution to every problem, and one day you will look back and laugh about this situation. I am sure you can recall a time in the past when you have experienced unbelievable worry and distress, whether it was a divorce, a loss of a loved one, a problem with a teenage child, or financial instability. Somehow you have indeed survived all of them, and should feel proud of how you have successfully dealt with each of the situation. All that we experience now brings with it a lesson to be learned, a lesson that can make us grow as stronger individuals. Problems can be attacked from different angles with different attitudes as well. Finding the best way to attack a problem with the least stress and pain is vital to keeping your peace.

# CHAPTER 20

# Fear: A State of Mind

> Thought impulses begin immediately to
> translate themselves into their physical
> equivalent, whether those thoughts are
> voluntary or involuntary.
> —*Napoleon Hill*

Fear is imagined insecurity. Any type of fear can affect you only if you allow it to. Fear has no power over a mind well equipped to topple any hurdle that gets in the way of success. You have control over what you want to imagine or think about. Be aware of your thought process. Know that you have the steering wheel of the car (your thoughts). You choose where you drive. The choice is within you. You are fully capable of conquering your fear.

Avoid thinking of your fears. Intensifying your fear with visualization allows the fear to become real. Imagining what you fear of most of the time will materialize the fear into your reality. This is what happens in the mind and imagination of a person constantly thinking of being afraid of experiencing poverty: he or she imagines how hard life would be when there is no money to pay for bills, almost feeling the hunger pangs that would be experienced due to the lack of food.

Then his or her mind keeps on going, now thinking about how pitiful the children will be without proper food to eat and no good clothes to wear. It goes on and on. This type of scenario played over and over in the mind that fears poverty, unconsciously invites poverty into life. The mind clouded with fear is unable to notice opportunities that can improve the situation. Your life becomes what you think of most often. Thinking of poverty gives you poverty.

## USE VISUAL IMAGERY

Think instead of riches and abundance! Then you shall have what you want as long as you want it bad enough. Train your mind to invite goodness into your life, imagining the comfort and fun of having enough and more. Think of how good it will feel to live in the home you have dreamed of. Imagine yourself relaxing under the summer sun by the poolside in your backyard. Think of the tastiest food that you can provide for your family. Picture the nice clothes that your money can buy. Now visualize having your dream car parked in your garage, just waiting for you to drive away with it. There is nothing wrong with being able to enjoy the perks in life that comes with your success.

Visualize the end as clearly as possible. Do not be distracted by worrying about what obstacles you may encounter on your way to acquiring what you want. When I went through a divorce with my first husband, I was at a loss. I was confused about what to do to take care of my son and my parents, who were dependent on me. My parents had just arrived from the Philippines and my dad had been diagnosed with lung cancer not too long after their arrival. I did not ask for anything in the divorce other than full custody of my son. I did not like courts and confrontations. All I wanted was to move on and start a new life. My son and I moved in with my parents, who were living in a two-bedroom basement apartment in Queens, New York. It was not easy in the beginning. I remember feeling bad when my six-year-old son asked me, "Mom why do we have to live under these people's house? Let us go back to Dad's house please." Those words cut through my heart.

Things got worse before they got better. I lost my job, and had to resort to collecting unemployment checks. There were times when there was no money to buy any food after I paid the rent, phone, and insurance for the car. On top of that, I got into a car accident that totaled my car. I was lucky to get out without a scratch. I told my son that our life could only get better. In my mind I told myself that all the hardship that I was experiencing was just temporary. I told myself, "I will survive and I will make it through." My philosophy was that I was able to make it in the Philippines, so I surely believed that I could make it in America. My faith, hope, and dreams kept me going as I seriously had to look deep into myself.

I asked myself, "What do I want? What can I do to get what I want? What immediate actions can help me better my situation?" Once I started looking in, I knew that I needed to take charge of my life. I needed to rally myself together and focus on my main responsibility as a mother to my son and a daughter to my parents. I also needed a change of environment. Somehow the fun of being single had blinded me from reality that I was compromising my financial life. I had not been seriously looking for a good job. I knew that I needed to totally turn myself around and change my focus to what truly mattered. What mattered most was my family. My brother had told me, "Bing, when things get too tough for you, come move in with my family in San Diego." So I called him and told him I was ready to take him up on his offer. I actually started packing our things and had already bought the cheapest ticket I could find before I called up my brother. Travel was a challenge especially with a young child and an elderly mother. Plus we had so many bags carried on and checked in. We looked like we have just evacuated from somewhere.

Around the same time, my friend Lisa and I would talk on the phone late into the night very often, expressing our dreams. I told Lisa that one day I hoped to find a stable job, meet a wonderful partner in life, and own a beautiful home with a nice backyard. We both would describe what our future homes would look like, from the hardwood floors to the winding stairs. Lisa would say, "I will visit you, Bing, and when I arrive at the door, I picture you coming down the stairs of your new home in a flowing pretty dress, smiling at me." In return, I would tell Lisa how I would visit her in her dream home, admiring the luxurious furnishings, the lavish garden, and the new car that she would own. We had long fun conversations like this about our dreams, even while we both lived very difficult lives at that moment.

Fast forward eight years: I had gotten remarried and I now live in the home that I share with my husband, Kevin, my son, Michael, and my mother, Luz. Lisa came to visit me as she promised. As she entered the door of my home, she became emotional. She had tears running down her face. We both looked at each other as if we had read each other's mind. Lisa hugged me tight and whispered, "Your dreams have come true, Bing." I said, "Yes Lisa, just as we have dreamed and pictured it, except I do not have the winding stairs." We laughed. Then I said, "Now I am living the dream." You too can one day live your dream.

Visual imagery is a powerful tool for you to use to invite abundance into your life. Visually seeing in your mind the images of how you want your life to be will change your reality drastically. Using the most descriptive imagery you can, close your eyes and see yourself living the most wonderful life you could ever want. What you want in your heart is what you have to think about as often as you possibly can throughout the day, like the intense obsession of a new love interest. You give your heart and thoughts to the one that you love. You have to do the same to the good life that you want. Write down everything you have imagined into your diary. Your new reality will become tangible; you are blowing life into this new world you have created. Remember that the more you have, the bigger your capacity to give to all those in need, and the stronger the impact you can have in lessening the suffering of other human beings.

You picked up this book in search for success and happiness now. What you need to do now, at this moment, is to have total mental, visual image control, which means that you get to pick positive internal pictures that project your inner intense desire for a great life. Positive visual images give birth to positive outcomes, eventually making success and happiness your true new reality.

## HOW TO FREE YOUR MIND OF FEAR

Consciousness of a strong spiritual core can enable you to repel all forms of fear. You have unlimited resources that you can tap for strength, guidance, creativity, and enlightenment. Imagine owning a remote control with a button that you can push to access the resources within you at any time that you want.

Use meditation to enhance your communication with the power within. There are audio books that you can buy or borrow from the library that can help you get started. Twenty minutes of meditation a day is a good start. You can progress to thirty minutes to an hour depending on your schedule. Tap into your inner self. You are complete and free. The resources within you are abundant. Meditation gets you in touch with your inner spirituality. The more often you meditate, the higher your state of awareness, the easier it is for you to tap into your inner resources throughout the day. When you live in total awareness and recognition of your gifts, repelling fears becomes as easy as throwing trash into the waste bin.

Fears can only stop you from gaining ground in acquiring the kind of life that you want for yourself. You do not have to be stuck in a world based on fear. Awareness of your complete control of your mind can open the gates to freedom from the bondage of your own created fears. You live in a world that you have created in your mind first. Anything that you are experiencing was formerly formulated in your head. Thoughts of fear that you allow to germinate in your mind eventually become a part of the world that you live in. Take responsibility for what type of thoughts you allow to dwell into your mind. Your mind is the factory where you create the kind of future you want for yourself. Do you want to manufacture a better life? Start by fertilizing positive thoughts, use affirmations to strengthen your resolve, and maintain total control of your mind.

## HOW CAN YOU GET RID OF THE FEAR OF FAILURE?

Success will never be a big step in the future, success is a small step taken just now.
— *Jonatan Martensson*

Fear of the unknown and untested waters is normal. As humans, we are comfortable with doing the things in life that are familiar. When there is familiarity, there is ease of mind. It is easier to live in a constant routine of familiar usual daily activities. However, if you want to be successful, you will need to get out of your comfort zone. Even when you fear, take the courage to take a calculated risk. According to Tehyi Hsieh, "Action will remove the doubts that theory cannot solve." Taking risks can sometimes generate fear, especially in the infant stages of an idea. But do not let your fear stop you from creating a wonderful future. Take the first step. You will be amazed of how things can escalate positively once you are able to take initial action.

Steps to Eliminate the Fear of Failure:

1. Acquire knowledge by researching and learning everything you can about the risk you want to take. Weigh the positive against the negative. Ponder and find ways to lower your risks. Knowledge becomes the foundation of courage. Your self-assurance increases as your fear diminishes.

2. Find mentors by surrounding yourself with men and women of wisdom who have paved the road ahead for you. The lessons they can teach you are priceless and they will provide you a better view of the road ahead. Their vision will lessen your fear and replace it with courage.

3. Muster courage to focus on the goal. Your positive vision of a progressive future builds your courage. Courage diminishes fear and replaces it with hope.

4. Be hopeful, as this will brighten up your path by giving you eager feelings about abundant times ahead. There is so much in life to hope for. Fill each present moment with the grace of hope.

5. Have great expectations and let them be for the best of what life has to offer. You are as good as you want yourself to be.

6. Take driven action. This is the key to jumpstart your performance. Action is the requirement to achieve your goal of success and happiness. Nothing will happen to your dreams unless you take the first step forward.

# CHAPTER 21

# Why Are Some People More Successful Than Others?

> The world we have created is a product of
> our thinking; it cannot be changed without
> changing our thinking.
>
> —*Albert Einstein*

The main difference between successful people and unsuccessful people is the quality of their thinking. Successful people have a crystal-clear vision of their future. They are constantly thinking of how they can make that vision happen and planning carefully each step of the way. Then they work with true determination to materialize the vision. Successful people are focused, optimistic, enthusiastic, and full of energy. They think and talk about their plans and their future. Their goals are defined. These people know exactly what they want; their goal is incredibly clear to them. Central to their state of mind is the knowledge that they will surely acquire their goal. It is just a matter of time before they get there.

Success-driven people glue their goals to their belief system with repetition. As if they had an obsession with a beautiful lover, these people passionately think of how it will feel when they finally can be with the object of their passion. Happily they pursue their goals, seemingly enjoying the challenges they undertake along the way.

Do you have a burning feeling in the core of your being exploding to take hold of what you desire most? Are you willing to do what it takes to make your desire become your reality? Are you willing to pay the price in the process of actually acquiring that which you want so badly? There is a price for everything you want. The question is, are you willing to spend time, effort, and money to get to where you want to be? Are you willing to learn what you have to do to make it happen? Are you committed to work hard with total faith to completely acquire what you want? Have you written actual plans that will take you closer to accomplishing this desire? Do you take action steps each day to make this desire into reality?

These are the questions to open up your mind. The first step to becoming successful is to finally put your desires on paper as goals, making them more tangible. Awaken your senses with that burning fire to convert your goals into organized plans and your plans into actual actions. Use a racehorse-like power to get you to the finish line. You can get what you want as long as you want it bad enough. The thirst for success will occupy your entire being, and you will become so driven that the vision of the finish line becomes very clear. All you need to do is keep the fire burning persistently until your desire becomes your true reality.

On the other hand, people who are not successful are preoccupied with the feeling of frustration and despair. They always find ways to complain about the weather, their job, and their lack of resources. They also find reasons to hate their boss and their neighbors, even their own body and life itself. There seems to be an endless list of daily complaints. Life for these people is a cycle of one unhappy event after another. When anything goes wrong, they blame others, but not themselves. They do not take responsibility for their actions. These individuals have thoughts that are so focused on negativity that they aggravate any situation. A dark cloud of gloom hangs over people who talk and think about negativity all day. Their energy is spent unwisely on a depressing outlook in life.

## CONTROL YOUR THOUGHTS TO CREATE A BETTER FUTURE

There are things in life that are out of your control: for instance, the weather, the winning numbers of the lottery, or the death of a loved one. With the weather, just accept the fact that it is a part of nature. Welcome the rain for its vital use, which is too vast to ignore. Plants, animals, and human beings can die without water.

If you are tempted to take chances on winning the lottery, try investing time instead in finding true luck by taking calculated risks in business. All you need is a great idea to find that first million dollars. Mix it with a burning desire. Plan for action. Then back up your actions with undying persistence. Persistence of the human spirit is what will ultimately bring you the abundance that you desire. Without persistence, all the potential that a human being possesses ceases development. Ideas will float in the air, remaining as wishes until someone else finds their vibrations and grabs them as an opportunity.

Once an idea finds a home in a mind that accepts no failure, it starts to develop and take a life of its own.

The death of a loved one is one of the hardest things for anyone to experience. It is beyond our control. We all wish to live forever if only we can also keep our youth with the passage of time. This planet earth might get way too crowded with young successful people if we had it our way. Remember that death is a part of life. We will one day experience it just as we all experience our birth into this world. Look at death as passing through to a different plane. It is the continuation of the journey of the spirit. Once our earthly mission is over, the soul is drawn back to the light of the One who is. Our spirit is ready for a new purpose.

To take control of your life, you need to take control of your future. The only way to take control of your future is to take control of your thoughts. You have sole ownership of your thoughts. No one can force you to think a certain way. As a sole navigator of the bus that is your mind, you can choose to stop and load it with only the passengers you want to occupy each prestigious seat. Imagine this bus as made of gold. It is precious, only special passengers are allowed on it.

There are a few special passengers that should always be on board. Make sure that Mr. Sunshine is on board to keep the upbeat enthusiasm of the group high. Let Miss Faith come aboard to solidify belief in oneself. As you know, thoughts are things that only belief has the magic to transform into reality. Be sure to let Mr. Hope entertain the group with uplifting jokes that lighten up the heart. Also welcome Miss Desire, Mr. Action, and Mr. Persistence. Here is how they interact when they show up:

All eyes are now on Miss Desire. She is one exotic, lovely, classy lady. Everyone turns their head. Each heart is captured with her intense fire. Make sure to have the fire extinguisher in the bus. Mr. Action chases the bus after seeing a glimpse of Miss Desire. Huffing and puffing, he pledges his love for her. Miss Desire, as attractive as she is, tells Mr. Action to get the large gold pot full of jewels buried in the sea of love. Mr. Action says, "I will get the large gold pot full of jewels as long as you promise to marry me and love me forever." Miss Desire answers with the sexiest, sweetest smile and says, "Go ahead my prince, take action immediately before any of my other suitors get to the gold pot of jewels ahead of you. I promise the first man to deliver it will take me as his bride." Mr. Action leaves in a hurry to find the treasure. On the way to the sea of love he takes hold of a diver named Mr. Persistence. Mr. Action pleads with Mr. Persistence for help to get to the treasure. Mr. Persistence agrees to help him in exchange for money. Mr. Action says, "Miss Desire is worth every penny that I will pay you." So both men sail the sea of love, persistently seeking the gold pot full of jewels. They dive non-stop for months, almost running out of supplies. Living off the fish they capture and drinking water from the rain that falls from the heavens, both men lose weight.

They became so weak. Mr. Action was losing it, almost ready to quit, crying for loss of energy and in physical pain. Mr. Persistence told him, "Oh be a man. Let us keep trying." Then, just as they were feeling too exhausted to do another search, Mr. Persistence comes out of the water with the gold pot full of jewels from the sea of love. Mr. Action pays Mr. Persistence a great amount of money for the help, and then proceeds to offer the gold pot full of jewels to Miss Desire. Miss Desire is happy and overwhelmed by love. Mr. Action and Miss Desire got married quickly and among the people invited were their best friends, Mr. Sunshine, Miss Faith, Mr. Hope, and, as the best man, Mr. Persistence. Mr. Action and Miss Desire bought an island that look like paradise and they live happily ever after.

## SUCCESSFUL PEOPLE FOCUS ON SOLUTIONS

> No matter where you go or what you do, you live your entire life within the confines of your head.
>
> —*Terry Josephson*

Do you want to be successful? Why not? With wealth you can enjoy the comfort of a beautiful life. With fortune you can enjoy precious time with your family. With money you can give generous contributions to your favorite charity. So wake up. Shake those sorry thoughts out of your mind. Focus your thoughts on finding solutions instead of focusing on the problems. Load your mind with the right passengers. Allow only the passengers we discussed above that can help you find success and happiness. Do not allow Mr. Negative, Miss Depression, Miss Poverty, or Mr. Whiner in your bus. It is your bus. You have the last word of who gets the ticket into this golden bus of your mind.

When you take control of the content of your mind, you take control of your life. Decide on success. Do not waste your time. Now is the perfect time. According to Henry Ford, "Obstacles are those frightful things you see when you take your eyes off your goal." Focus on your goal. Imagine yourself climbing up a ladder. Do not keep looking down or the height will scare you. Keep your eyes on the end result. Concentration plus the quality of your thoughts can help to create a clear vision of your future. Your clear vision can guide you to set your goals. Your goals can direct your actions to acquire the ideal life that you want.

Write down your goals. Write long-term goals. What do you want to have achieved in ten years? What you want to have achieved in five years? You can also write what you want to have achieved in a year, a month, or within the week. Seeing your goals written on paper helps to bring them to life. Your list becomes a real plan. Planning is the key. Navigate life with a written plan. You will set yourself a higher degree of standard than the average person who has no written contract to succed. It is not enough to talk about your dreams. Words are fleeting when not put down in ink. They fly out into space and dissipate. Then they are forever forgotten.

My husband and I encourage each other to write our individual goals on index cards. We often discuss our goals together as we relax on our deck having a glass of wine or while we cooked on the grill. We have a large board that we share on which to pin the goals that we have written. I pin my goals in the left area of the board, and the right side is for his goals. We hang our goal board on the wall next to our sink at the powder room, which works out well because we get to glance at it while we get ready in the morning. Every few months, we update our goal board, which is fun to do. We take off the index cards of the goals we have achieved and celebrate as we replace them with new goals we want to pursue.

A clear vision with a written goal can energize your body to take action. Intent becomes crystallized into action. Your actions can yield positive results. Action with passion can make things happen. Action paired with relentless persistence has magnified results, results that seem miraculous to the naked eye. Unseen vibrating positive forces can bring you success.

Success can give you comfort. Never having to worry about money again will give you ample time to enjoy the things that you want to do, like spending more time with your loved ones. You can also start bigger philanthropic missions to help others in the areas you are passionate about. Success gives you the freedom to use your time the way that you want to. You can still choose to keep working, though you do it for the love of it. When you are successful enough, you work because you enjoy the challenge of waking up with a purpose and because working can keep your mind sharp. But you are not a slave to your job or business. Work is something fun to do when you want to.

Successful people are:
- Visual
- Optimistic
- Energetic
- Action oriented

Unsuccessful people are:
- Constantly blaming others
- Obsessed with negative thoughts
- Drained of energy

# CHAPTER 22

## Thought Is the Seed for Success, Power, and Wealth

> Flaming enthusiasm, backed up by horse
> sense and persistence, is the quality that
> most frequently makes for success.
>
> —*Dale Carnegie*

My son Michael is a young entrepreneur. When he was nine, I began giving him books to read. Our deal was that for every book he read, he was able to collect twenty dollars as a reward after he passed an oral test, which usually happened around the dining table at dinner. This went on for several years. Michael did not get any cash allowances so that was the only way he made some cash.

I started mentoring my son at a young age to learn about business. I picked books that taught him about financial responsibility, management, real estate, Internet business and more. I often spoke to him about how important it was to become financially responsible at a young age so that he could have the opportunity to retire young and be able to enjoy life. I advised him to pursue his interests while owning his own business. I often said to him, "Michael when you have your own business, you make money that goes into your pocket; when you work for someone else you put more money into someone else's pocket."

When Michael turned fourteen years old, we moved to Albany, New York. I continued to mentor him, discussing business, work ethic, and financial responsibility. I told him some mistakes I had made when I got through my divorce, like how I got myself into debt by not having been attentive to my finances. By letting my son know where I had gone wrong, I tried to teach him how he could prevent himself from making the same mistakes.

One day as I was busy painting the basement, Michael came downstairs with a serious look in his face. He said, "Mom, I have a great idea to start a business but I am too young. Can you cosign for me to get an account with eBay?" I kept on painting, thinking that he was not serious about what. he was saying. Oh, was I wrong. Michael got so frustrated that I was not giving him the time of day. He raised his voice at me, saying, "Mom listen to me! For so many years you have made me read all those business books and now that I have a business idea you are not listening to me." Those words stopped me in my tracks. I said, "OK, let me hear it all."

After Michael explained to me his desire to open an account with eBay, I asked him what it was that he planned to sell? He said, "Mom, I can sell all the books and anything that you don't need from the storage area of our basement." I said, "After you finish selling what we have in the basement, what are you going to sell?" Michael said that he would ask his friends if they had any old games and stuff that they didn't want so he could sell it on eBay for a profit. Then I continued to ask my son, "After you have sold all that, what are you going to sell next?" Michael replied, "I don't know." "Well that is what you need to know before I cosign anything for you," I answered.

I told my son that he had to make a study. He needed to get familiar with the products being sold in eBay. Then he needed to find wholesale suppliers with the products that caught his interest. I gave him a notebook and pen and a calculator. I told my son whatever product he chose, to make sure that it was unique with great profit potential. I was amused to see my son at work. He was so focused on his research on the Internet for at least two weeks. Every now and then he would show me the picture of a product and the possible income it could make for him if he bought it wholesale. He was serious, focused, and determined, so I started paying closer attention. When I felt he was ready I cosigned a checking account so he could set up Paypal, and then I opened the eBay account. I gave him $275 to start and told him, "Show me what you can do with this money. Grow it, make some profit and learn. You will have many mistakes, but never stop doing business just because at some point you fail. Get up after every fall. If you want to succeed, you can never give up. Make sure that your inventory keeps on moving."

My son is 17 years old as I am writing this book. He has rolled the small money I gave him as capital into thousands of dollars. He is a power seller, and has 100 percent positive feedback with his business. I am so proud of him. He takes very good care of his customers, does quality checks on his products before sending them out promptly, and addresses any concerns immediately. Michael is entering college in the fall and will continue to do business through the Internet while he is at school studying to become an engineer. I am confident that the lessons he acquires now as a young man will carry on to take him where he wants to be in the future. One thing I made sure to reiterate to my son was that I want him to do what he wants to do, what is in his heart, to go to school for what interests him and not what interests me. I encourage my readers who have children to help cultivate their children's imagination, to get them started thinking of all the unlimited possibilities of what they can do. Thought can give birth to ideas that when captured, used, and executed can make a big difference in life.

## THE SEEDS OF SUCCESS

Success starts as an internal seed, a seed thirsty for growth. Thoughts are seeds of life. Good thoughts are healthy seeds that bear the abundant fruit of a great life. Bad seeds are negative thoughts that can only bear the rotten, unhealthy outcome of a life of poverty, unhappiness, and deprivation. Think of yourself as a farmer, fertilizing the ground where the seed grows. The seed will sprout in the most conducive environment. If you are an experienced farmer, you will weed out the bad seeds of negative thoughts and not allow them to grow in your garden of life (your mind). Cultivating the good seeds with desire and positive imagery will allow them to grow. Planting the seed of success will lead to a harvest of the fruit of inspired action. Your well-directed inspired actions will give you a life of happiness and abundance.

You do not have to be rich to become rich. A lot of people who acquired wealth came from humble beginnings. Examples are Thomas Edison, Henry Ford, Oprah Winfrey, and Andrew Carnegie. What these people have in common is the burning desire to achieve greater heights. Their excessive passion accelerated their actions to take them to the top. Therefore, the circumstances of your life must not be used as an excuse to stop you from growing, succeeding, and attaining happiness. Your success is not dependent on the circumstances of your life. Success is gained after you have made a commitment to take charge of your destiny. You can create the circumstances. You can create your own opportunities, through the awareness of your complete control of your most precious property, your very own mind.

Whether you are young, middle age, or older, everyone has equal chance to succeed. The person who has mastered the total control of the power of the mind is the one who will reach success no matter what age. According to Napoleon Hill, people around the ages of forty and sixty years of age have been known to achieve more success. Experience is indeed a very good teacher. Awakening of wisdom happens when a person can focus. Youth comes with accelerating fun, discovery, and sexual experiences. There is not much energy left for things to explore after exhaustion. Be glad for your wisdom, use it to open possibilities for you.

## SET A DEADLINE FOR YOUR SUCCESS

A specific deadline that you set for reaching your goal makes the finish line become more visible. Have a precise figure that you want to earn at a particular time. Write down in ink on an index card the date of when you want this goal to happen. Seeing it in writing is like having a contract with your own self. It becomes a defined time that is fed into your subconscious mind of when you expect things to materialize. Setting a date can make your dream tangible.

Make sure to read your index card in the morning when you get up and at night before you go to bed. Repeating this information to yourself as often as you can throughout the day is vital to feeding this information into your subconscious mind. Soon enough the information becomes a part of your own beliefs. Once you believe, the universe will have no other way but to grant you what you want. Opportunities will start emerging. Brilliant ideas will start to come to the surface.

Most great success comes from an idea whose potential an inspired person recognized. Planning then had to take place to bring this idea to life. The only way to make an idea into a reality is to take action. Pluck the idea from your thoughts by doing something about it. Your thoughts remain only a place to dream until you allow them to guide your actions into formulating ways to mold the dream into your true living world.

Think about it: if all you do is daydream all day, lying in bed wishing for your dreams to happen, how will that make a difference in the way you live your life now? You will stay in the same situation for as long as you lie there doing nothing. However, if you choose to use your thoughts as the birthplace of success, power, and wealth, you can derive energy from within for guided action. The secret is in the constant movement forward. No amount of dreaming can make things happen if you are not willing to pay the price for what you want. Keep on doing, keep on moving, keep your head up and expect the best.

## VISION IS POWER

> Success is the achievement of a desired goal through persistence, enduring countless obstacles along the way while focusing on a great vision.
>
> —*Bing Wilson*

The picture that you hold in your mind is vital for success. Picture yourself in a world that you want, with a happy, fulfilling home life and a job that challenges your creative faculties as well as providing well for your needs and the needs of your family. Envisioning what you want can affect the physical senses of the body as if you have already acquired your goal. A vision of a great future increases your desire for it, attracting that which you so dearly want. Increasing the intensity of the desire brings out your passion for actual action.

Crystal-clear visualization of the foreseen future becomes an instrument of faith. You may not know how you will get there, but you know you will one day be there because right at this very moment you know exactly how it feels to achieve your dream. You are feeling the emotions of living the dream, conditioning your mind and body to be ready for reality to play itself. Constant positive thoughts and visions are consuming your mind, fusing into your belief system.

Success seems to be largely a matter of
hanging on after others have let go.
—*William Feather*

## FOCUSING ON NEGATIVE
## THOUGHTS BRINGS FAILURE

Imagining negativities and taking in sad and depressing
information feeds your subconscious mind the information
at its face value, as if it is the reality that you want. The
subconscious mind does not know right from wrong. It
just records these pictures and feelings as if they are what
you desire. A person can get himself or herself into deeper
depression by constantly berating his or her own capacity,
making it worse. A person suffering from financial hardships
who cannot stop talking about how tough life is and blaming
the whole world about his or her tough reality without taking
responsibility also makes his or her situation worse.

Life is a matter of choice. If you constantly think of
your lack of love, lack of money, and lack of happiness,
brewing a deep resentment against the world because of
your misfortune, life will simply get worse for you. Focusing
on the negative attracts depressing sad, traumatic events,
becoming a self-fulfilling prophecy. Thinking about the
frustrations of the problems compounds the problem even
more. Do you really want to make it worse for yourself?

It is your responsibility to feed your mind with thoughts
that can take you out of your rut. Carefully feed your mind
the vision and information of what you really want in your

heart. Focus on the solutions instead of the obstacle at hand. Imagine how much better it will be when you apply solution A, B, or C to a problem. For each problem you encounter, provide as many solutions you can find.

You can think of ways to expand the love you receive by thinking of good possible gestures of love you can give to another human being. You cannot expect to get a lot of love when you do not consciously give love as much as you can at every opportunity that you can find.

If the problem is money, ask yourself about ways of improving your value at work. Volunteer to do more than what you are being paid to do with utmost sincerity and enthusiasm. Take courses or seminars that can make you grow in the industry you are in, giving you a better edge compared to the rest. Dare to be different in a positive way. Do you think a search for a new job can increase your income? Are you afraid of the unknown? If you change your spending habits, will it help your financial situation?

Is a lack of happiness frustrating you? Do you believe that happiness is coming from your outer environment that you are only here waiting for it to happen? Happiness is an internal personal decision that you make with yourself. If you decide to be happy, no one can stop you. You are a co-creator of your own living present reality. You are responsible for making happiness radiate from within you. Happiness is an attitude, a way of seeing life with utmost optimism. Imagine reaching your desired outcome vividly. The more vivid the picture you have, the easier it will be for you to resolve the problem. When you allow negativity to occupy your mind, it is as if you are inviting and welcoming dark forces into your life. Negativity diminishes your energy, lessening your ability to have power to acquire success in life.

> Thought is the wind, knowledge the sail, and mankind the vessel.
> —*Augustus William Hare and Julius Charles Hare,*
> from *Guesses at Truth, by Two Brothers,* 1827

## QUALITY OF THOUGHT PRODUCES QUALITY ACTION

As you hold that clear vision of what you desire in your mind, you gain power through the awareness of your ability to choose what thoughts and information you allow to be absorbed in your subconscious mind, choosing only those that will produce a multitude of successes. Govern your thoughts to cultivate a high quality of thinking. The quality of your thoughts can be improved by continuously thirsting for knowledge. For as long as life continues, education must continue to shape your world. New information is like breathing in fresh air full of hope that no matter what problem you will encounter, you seem to know that there is a way to solve it. Wisdom prepares you before embarking on a venture as it enables you to make wise sensible decisions. Each decision paves the way to your dreams.

Your positive thoughts, strong conviction and faith can push you into well guided actions. Your driven actions can deliver results. Results can only happen after action has taken place. Keep on moving. When there is no movement, there is no progress to expect. Fuel your movement with the persistence of a bull. Success is just a few inches away from the man who gives up. The next person to take over the task will be the lucky one. Regrets will come too late. Arm your actions with the seal of undying persistence and you will achieve far more successes than anyone can possibly imagine.

## WEALTH IS THE BONUS OF ACHIEVING SUCCESS

What is wealth? Wealth can mean different things to different people. Some people feel wealthy when they have great health and good enough income to take care of their daily needs. For others wealth is when they have accumulated compounding investments that give them freedom of time. Why do people search for financial freedom? Is it mainly for the purpose of paying their bills on time? Is it because they want the best home, car, and clothes that money can buy?

All the above are just the extras: what financial freedom can truly give is time. A person with wise investment choices can do more fun things with his or her time. Smart investing involves building compounding wealth, making money work for you over time instead of you chasing it. Your money gives birth to new interest even when you are spending quality time with your family or playing golf with your friends.

Wealth is the materialization of your big vision into your reality. Wealth is the grand accumulation of profit from ideas, businesses, stocks, and real estate. For wealth to bring financial freedom, it must be enough to allow the person possessing it to enjoy all the usual pleasures of life even when he or she decides to stop working. According to Robert Kiyosaki, author of *Rich Dad, Poor Dad,* "Wealth is nothing more than a measurement of time. It is how long you can continue to live your lifestyle without any adjustments when you cease working." Time is wealth, a very precious commodity. It can be awesome when a person is able to own his or her time and enjoy life fully.

How can one own his or her time fully? It all starts as a commitment to succeed. Success is truly driven by the love of freedom. Freedom from the bondage of a routine like work, freedom from living paycheck to paycheck, freedom from working for someone else. Once a seed of freedom is planted in the subconscious mind of a person, success is imminent. Needing to acquire wealth is the price of the persevering, burning passion for the goal of being free.

As your mind begins to master the art of ruling your thoughts, you are able to program your mind to seek only success, overcoming obstacles, keeping your mind focused on the goal, and using desire to fire up your actions while persevering to get to where you want to be. Once your first success is achieved, many more doors will open to even more opportunities. Once financial abundance pours in, it pours in like a river flowing. You will be amazed, as you reach the top of the game, how things come to you effortlessly.

Even if at some point in your life you lose everything, you know that you can get up and reclaim the success you have lost. Wealth building is character building. The more compassionate you are toward others, the better will be your family and social relationships that you need to support you in your endeavor. The more loving you are, the more love that you get back, giving you a warm feeling of comfort, The kinder you are, the more abundance flows into your life. Wealth combined with health and a great family relationship is very rewarding. What is money when along the way as you accumulated it, you ruined your health? Live a healthy lifestyle so that you can enjoy the fruit of your success. What is wealth when the family is in turmoil? Remember to put your family first. Your loved ones are the main reason why you work hard to get to where you are, that you may provide a good life for them. What is freedom of time when you do not have anyone to enjoy it with? Cultivate your family and personal relationships along the way to your goal of success. Success is sweeter when you can share it with people you love. It gets even better when you can actively experience freedom of time with a healthy body.

Success is achieved by:
- Setting goals
- Creating a great vision
- Having good intention behind each action
- Maintaining strong belief
- Expanding knowledge
- Take action

Write down your goals. This is a contract you have with yourself for success. Write as many as you want in present tense. Keep rewriting it until you get it down to what you want. Make sure to put them in order of importance.

1. _____
2. _____
3. _____
4. _____
5. _____
6. _____
7. _____
8. _____
9. _____
10. _____

Describe the great vision you have in your mind. Be as creative and as colorful as you can. Your clear vision will help in bringing the picture to life. Feel the emotion as if you are experiencing it now

_____
_____
_____
_____
_____
_____
_____
_____
_____
_____
_____

What type of knowledge and skills do you need to acquire to increase your speed in acquiring success?

_____

_____

_____

_____

_____

_____

_____

_____

_____

_____

_____

_____

_____

What action steps can you do to get you started in your journey to success?

1. _____

2. _____

3. _____

4. _____

5. _____

6. _____

7. _____

8. _____

9. _____

10. _____

# CHAPTER 23

## Powerful Thinking Creates Results

You and I are not what we eat; we are what
we think.
—*Walter Anderson, The Confidence Course,*
1997

I have grown up in the Philippines under challenging conditions. We were very poor. After the separation of my parents I learned to help my mother and my brother make a living by tending to our small deli until the late hours of the night. I was only 9 years old and my brother 12. My mother kept us strong together. Her dream, which she communicated to us, was that my brother and I succeed in our studies. She told us how important it was for us to get a good education. My mother had so much conviction in her voice when she spoke to us. She worked so hard to raise us and we respected and loved her and only want to do what can please her.

Why do I point out to you the hard life I experienced in the past? To inspire you that no matter what happened in your past, your mind can help you change your situation in life. There is hope. Key to getting what you want to succeed is the use of the power of your thinking mind to give you freedom from any limitations of your environment and any limitations that you have given yourself prior to awakening to the new reality. A boundless exciting life of health, wealth, success and happiness can follow.

Powerful thinking revs up your performance engine an extra notch, creating a forceful, well-directed movement to accomplish the task of creating a new reality. It is the focused-thinking mind that generates the energy, dissecting complex of problems into smaller focused parts, making it simpler to understand how to direct actions accordingly.

Thinking increases your creativity. Used effectively, it enables the mind to render importance to ideas, which will maximize rewards in the future. Thinking helps you find answers to countless questions. In the quiet moments of deep thought are found profound solutions to problems. Look within to find the way. A powerful-thinking mind is the guiding force behind each effective action. Actions follow the course formerly rehearsed in the thoughts. Assessments of courses of action can be done over and over in the thoughts until confidence arises. Your confidence minimizes mistakes. Your ability to run through a scenario in your mind many times enables you to see your path clearly, eliminating mistakes by foreseeing obstacles ahead of time.

Powerful thinking is the root cause of the elaborate triumph of successful people. Effective action follows the driven, powerful-thinking mind. The body goes in full throttle to do what the mind has pursued in thoughts over and over. It is therefore important to cultivate powerful creative thinking to keep the body moving forward closer to its ultimate goal.

Powerful thinking gives you energy as well as purpose. It can enable you to make things happen quicker. Your increased velocity toward your goal decreases the time it takes to reach your dream of success. Confidence is acquired through the thinking process. Confidence can give you power: power to enhance your present reality, power to put into action what your thoughts have resolved to do to achieve success, power to see beyond the present and foresee the future in the mind's eye.

## THE MIND IS A GREAT TOOL FOR SUCCESS

The mind is a powerful tool that can guide your life. A positive mental attitude is derived from the awareness that this special tool is in you. Your mind is the throne of your inner core. It is where the seed of life hibernates. Fertilize your mind with what it needs to fuel your senses with positive energy. It all starts in your head: ideas, beliefs, dreams, and possibilities. An uplifting thought can increase your physical energy, awakening the life source of unlimited power into action. It increases the sensitivity of all your other senses. You can almost feel it, you can almost smell it, you can almost touch it. Success is in the palm of your hand. Discover that you are complete, because you are a part of perfection. The energy of life in you is perfect and eternal.

Allow a time during the day for a quiet dreamtime. Dream big: it will not cost you any money. Dreaming and imagining allow you to foresee your future the way that you want it if you were to have it your way without limitation. When you truly believe in yourself, your dreams can materialize into your life. You can become an unstoppable positive force. Your energy and enthusiasm can bring out the best qualities in you. You start recognizing that you have what it takes to get to wherever you want to be.

By now you can understand how important it is to protect your mind. Let go of thoughts that are limiting. Limiting thoughts reduce your energy. They can bring you darkness, depression, and failure. A negative thought can pull you away from your dreams. It can only bring you down.

Exercise mental discipline. Be vigilant with what thoughts you entertain. Treat your mind like a jewel. It has timeless value. Give it what it deserves. Allow it to spark to light your path to success. There is a direct relationship between your mental state and your physical being. When you choose to eat nourishing food, it makes you mentally alert and physically healthy. Add exercise as a part of your life, and you will build a strong body to support that well-functioning mind.

A strong mind is not withered by the challenges that life presents. It derives its strength from the constant mental calisthenics of finding solutions to the various problems that arise. The mind becomes alert and aware that there are hidden solutions to problems. Searching for solutions becomes a challenge that stimulates the mind. It is your mental strength that can keep you going. If one path does not take you to the answer, you move on to an alternative path. When you stumble, get up; do not stop to feel sorry for yourself. Self-pity can only deplete you of energy. Dwell instead on the countless possibilities in order to unlock the tremendous gift of your inner creativity.

Cultivate your mental power. Understanding the power

of your mind can help you understand why you are in the situation that you are in now. What are the thoughts that dominate your mind from the time you get up in the morning until the time you go to bed at night? Do you wake up looking forward to the day ahead? Are you grateful for the gift of life? Do you fill your thoughts with positive enthusiasm for being alive? Do you feel good knowing that each day is a chance to learn something new? Does each moment present a new opportunity to make a difference in the world that you live in? Are you going through the day with a smile and joy in your heart? Do you go to bed grateful and satisfied for all the experiences that allowed you to grow throughout the day?

Your thoughts dictate the kind of day you will have. You can have a beautiful day when you decide that each day will be as wonderful as you imagine it to be, that nothing can hamper your happiness unless you allow it to. If you start your day by dragging yourself out of bed complaining about the rain outside your bedroom window and then dreading the drive to work, then you set a negative tone for the day. You have allowed yourself to be distracted from creating a happy joyful day. You get down to the kitchen already overwhelmed before your breakfast, then you burn your toast and spill your coffee on yourself. Can you imagine what the rest of the day will be like?

I want to remind you once again that happiness is a state of mind. Start your day right by using positive thoughts that can give you energy and enthusiasm for the day. Do not allow the negative thoughts to creep in. Use your awareness to build a shield against negative thoughts, negative impulses, and negative influence from others. Have the willpower to reject unhealthy thoughts. You can only be truly happy when you learn to be the navigator of your own mind. You are strong enough that no storm can collapse your will. No limiting thoughts are allowed to dwell too long in your precious mind.

How Can I Use My Mind as a Tool for Success?
- Choose a positive mental attitude
- Have a quiet dreamtime each day
- Exercise mental discipline
- Recognize the connection between mind, body, and soul
- Recognize your mental power

How Can Powerful Thinking Create Results?
Powerful Thinking Can:
- Give you a great vision for the future
- Help discover your true purpose
- Increase your performance
- Increase creativity
- Eliminate mistakes
- Guide your actions
- Create energy
- Strengthen your confidence

❦

# CHAPTER 24

## Cultivating Your Imagination
## to Achieve Success

Paint a world of wonder in your mind until
you find yourself in it.

*—Bing Wilson*

Developing a healthy imagination is essential in achieving success. Imagination plants the seed in the subconscious mind. Pretend that you are an inventor of the highest degree. You are on a mission to create a life pattern that suits how you imagine life should be if you had it all. Picture yourself in the area of work that will best give you the most satisfaction in life. Imagine how you will carry your image. You can imagine, for example, yourself dressed very dignified, conducting business at a very profitable firm that you own. As you get out of work, you happen to be driving your red Porsche to get home. Feel the emotions as you finally arrive at your dream home. The happy faces of your children greet you as you enter through the carved oak door. Now you can finally relax in your backyard by the poolside, spending time with your family.

Imagine in your mind the desired outcome for every goal in the most colorful way. Your clear quality of vision has a direct link to how you feel now and the way your days unfold ahead. Use your vision to take you closer to the goal. Focus on developing an imagination full of positive visual content that represents your passion for the betterment of life. Combine your imagination with continuous movement forward and you will feel as if you have arrived at the goal. Feel the exhilarating excitement of being at the top and feel the triumph of winning the game. Taste the pleasure of being a winner. What you think about most often eventually becomes a part of your environment.

> A rock pile ceases to be a rock pile the
> moment a single man contemplates it,
> bearing within him the image of a cathedral.
> —*Antoine de Saint-Exupery,*
> *Flight to Arras,* 1942

## MIND DISCIPLINE

Apply discipline in developing positive visual stimulus in your mind's eye. Guard your mental vision against negative imagination. The society that we live in is bombarded with negative, sad information from the news to television programs that are all over the networks. The news media dramatizes heavily on the emotional drama and trauma of the events that they cover. The public loves the drama, so the media keeps feeding them what they seek. As we keep ourselves glued to the tube showing the nonstop violence of the war on the streets as well as the wars in different areas of the world, our minds are overloaded with depressing information. Watching the news for several hours a day can make you feel as if the world is falling apart at its edges. Naturally, we share this information with our loved ones and colleagues. Now the emotions spread for all to experience and the pain is compounded. Going through the day we feel sadness, irritability and frustration.

Notice the demeanor of the people around you. Why do we see many long faces? The look of people burdened by bricks of hardships on their backs. Negative information is draining. Allowing an excessive bombardment of this type of information to consume your mind is not healthy. You create a dense barrier that hinders your mind from functioning effectively for the purpose of elevating your way of life. Negative imaginings can give you stress and discomfort. Stress is draining; it will not help you to improve your situation. Thinking and imagining negative thoughts can draw this negativism to happen in your life.

What you truly want is success and happiness. Make a decision to be easy on yourself. Imagine and visualize vividly what you desire in your heart. Inspiring vision gives you energy, giving you fuel for forward movement. Forward movement is important in achieving success.

## HAVE FAITH

Believe that your goal is attainable. Ask yourself, "How can I make it happen?" Positive self-talk paves the way toward the beginning of your journey. Refrain from saying phrases such as, "It is impossible," "I can never make it," or "There is no way it can happen." This type of negative self-talk shuts the door for you. It is an unconscious negation of what you want. Rid your mind of doubts quickly by eliminating negative self-talk in exchange for positive affirmations. Tell yourself that it is just a matter of time until you figure out a way. Faith strengthens the will to go after your dreams no matter what.

Do not be impatient about figuring out the "how"; the "how" will present itself eventually. What is important is that you believe that what you are pursuing is possible. Your ability to foresee what you want in your mind increases your passion within.

Emotions triggered by the picture you hold in your mind can set the stage for your goals to happen. What you believe deeply will materialize. Focus your mind's eye on the prize, then pursue it with utmost driven desire. The intensity of your faith will make miracles for you. You are what you think you are; what is in your mind most often will find a way into your life. Your thoughts allow hope to increase, and hope strengthens your faith. It takes power from within you to take action. Believe in yourself, accept the reality that you can achieve anything that you want.

If, on the other hand, you keep talking about something you do not have enough of, like money or time with your family, the problem compounds. Verbalizing alone cannot solve the problem. Recognize the problem, then imagine how nice it would be to have it the other way. Ask yourself, "How would I feel if I had all the money that I need plus the quality time to spend with my loved ones?" Start planting the seed of the solution by imagining the opposite of the problem.

Germination happens as you start to feel the emotions of the desire. Constantly imagining success, aided by written plans and affirmations, will materialize your goals. What you toy with in your mind becomes what you play with in real life. The potential within you is beyond limit. Tap into your inner core for unlimited power.

What you feed your mind is just as important as what you feed your body. Your thoughts can recreate your environment. There is no limit to your creative imagination. Allow your imagination to entertain positive possibilities. You do not need a high IQ to become successful. It can help, but it is not the main factor. A successful person has the burning fire in his or her soul. This person believes that anything is possible. With great vision this person gives the best in each performance of skill and application of knowledge.

## FOCUS ON THE SOLUTIONS

When problems arise in business or your personal life, focus on the solution. Use your energy to make optimistic solutions and movement toward productivity. Expect the best, imagine the best, and work toward creating extraordinary results. Keep your imagination alive. The fire within you increases. Let your movement be brisk as you move forward. Imagine vividly and act passionately with the fire from within you to reach success.

> The man who acquires the ability to take
> full possession of his own mind may take
> possession of anything else to which he is
> justly entitled.
>
> —*Andrew Carnegie*

## BIGGER DREAMS FOR GREATER SUCCESS

Stimulate your mind with bigger dreams for the future. Be creative, this exercise will not cost you anything.

I was at a doctor's office one day. While waiting for the nurse to come in, I kept myself busy reading the book *Your Magic Power to Be Rich* by Napoleon Hill. When the nurse, Mimi, entered, she noticed the book and proceeded to ask if it was good. I told her it was awesome and inspirational. We hit it off quickly. She told me that she has viewed the movie *The Secret* three times, and told me how she was trying to apply it to her life.

So I asked Mimi what was it that she truly wanted to happen in her life to make her happy. Mimi told me that she would be happy and content if she could have a little bit more money so that she could pay the bills and go on vacation with her family at least once a year. I then told Mimi that if that is all that she wants then that is exactly what she will get, and no more. I encouraged her to dream for more.

It does not matter what it is that you want. It does not matter how much of it you want. What matters is the intensity of how much you want it when you ask for it. Do not be afraid to ask for utmost abundance. Why put a cap on your horizon? The heavens are wide open with unlimited resources for those who have mastered the ability to ask for what it is that they need with conviction.

## PERSISTENCE PAYS

Pursue your goals without ceasing. Let no obstacles or failures stop you. Gather your strength and pick up the pieces. Keep on trying. Do not ever give up. Success is not instantaneous. It is a process of moving forward after each failure until you arrive at your goal. It is necessary to have a strong mind. Unrelenting persistence is the key to ultimately achieve success. Learn from your failures, but do not dwell on them. Do not give up. Move forward with faith. Keep pushing. There is nothing impossible when your vision is clear.

> Success isn't a result of spontaneous
> combustion. You must set yourself on fire.
> —*Arnold H. Glasow*

Life is all about the choices. You are the one to live within the confines of each decision that you make throughout your life. Do not imprison yourself within the imaginary limitations in your head. You are as good as you want, as bad as you allow, as gifted as you like, as successful as you desire to be. So choose to excel. Success is a matter of decision to never fail. A successful individual is one who has learned and mastered how to acquire his or her goals with focused passionate imagination.

Loving what you do is vital for success. Pour your soul

into a pure interest and love for the task. Lose yourself in an activity that you strongly desire. Work becomes effortless. It will equal fun. Creativity expands and surfaces when you are happily pursuing your goal. Your productivity brings you closer to success.

Cultivate Imagination Through:
- Constancy of positive thoughts
- Focusing on the solution
- Having big dreams
- Feeling the emotions from the vision

# CHAPTER 25

## Acquire Knowledge for Growth

The purpose of learning is growth, and
our minds, unlike our bodies, can continue
growing as we continue to live.

*—Mortimer Adler*

When I was about 34 years old, my thirst for knowledge became very intense. It may have come from maturity and wanting to better myself. I became obsessed with reading educational materials that interested me. Going to the library for me was like going to the candy store. I learned about real estate from the dozens of books I borrowed and purchased, and shared the knowledge with my husband Kevin while we were still dating, which made our phone conversations very long! We had a long distance relationship. In the four years that Kevin and I dated, he fell asleep once or twice while we were on the phone. But he survived.

I continued to read about psychology and behavioral sciences. I was curious about the mystery of the mind. I believe that there is so much more that science will discover in the future about the human mind. I studied biographies of successful people and learned what habits and actions helped them achieve success. I read spiritual books and books on self-improvement. Understanding myself is very important for me in learning to improve my relationships with others. For fun, I also studied how to read palms. It is amazing how much the lines in the palm of the hand can tell about the basic traits of a person. I had a good time reading my friends' palms. It made for a lot of laughter. I mostly read the good stuff off the hands, as I did not want to be the bearer of bad news.

Looking back, my thirst for knowledge has always been there. When I was 16 years old and getting ready to go to college, there were no financial institutions advertising to lend money to students. I don't know if they existed in the Philippines at that time. They did have scholarships. When I asked the principal at St. Theresa's College about the possibility of my getting some sort of scholarship for my studies, she told me that if I decided to take education as my major, I could get a full four years paid for by the school as long as I signed a contract to work for the school afterwards for several years. Becoming a school teacher did not appeal to me. My mother was a grade school teacher, and I had sat in many of her classes and saw a lot of the frustrations she had with her young students.

I followed my heart. I wanted to take communication arts, so I opted to find a way to pay for school. Once I came up with the idea to learn how to sew dresses, I placed all my energy into the task. Aside from learning the sewing trade, I thought that if I could design the clothes that my customers wanted, I would be able to get more business. The funny thing was that I never had a talent in drawing. I could hardly draw anything decent enough to be called art but I told myself, "I can do it." I kept telling myself, "I will learn to design and sew clothes," over and over. Day and night I kept drawing clothes for weeks, and amazingly the drawings got better and better. I designed casual wear, evening gowns, uniforms and wedding clothing. My mother taught me how to make the basic patterns for clothes in one day. She sat down with me, and I absorbed the information and took a lot of notes. As time went on, I would consult her if I needed clarification on some work. Otherwise it was trial and error in the beginning. I did not have the full knowledge, but I was determined to go for it and learned the rest as I went on.

My knowledge quest and persistence succeeded. It was just my mom and I doing the work at the start, but after a few months the work became too overwhelming. I had to hire dressmakers, eight to ten at a time. I bought used sewing machines, and the work was all done in the basement apartment where we used to live. My customers were my schoolmates, office workers, nurses, hotel workers, and entertainers. Word got around as I went door to door as well. It was a pretty hectic lifestyle. Being a full-time college student and running a business in full swing was not easy. I am proud to say that I was never late in paying my tuition fees, and made so many friends in the process. Customers confided in me about their personal life when they visited. I felt like a mentor to so many people, giving them advice and a shoulder to cry on. Visits became long at times, but I did not mind. It was important to build good relationships with my customers. The more trust I gained, the more they kept coming back to use my products.

Knowledge is the key to eradicating fear. Once acquired, new information increases your confidence to take the next step to unlock great possibilities, leading you to unlimited power to improve your life. With the key in your hand, take action to find the right door that fits the key.

What brings the positive changes in your life lies in your ability to put the knowledge that you have accumulated into a well-defined action plan. Once you have written the plan, study it, and then embark on the mission of finding the right keyhole that fits the key in your possession. Lack of formal education will not keep you from success. Success is born from inspired actual action. Knowing where you can find the information you need is more crucial.

If you need to know how to do something, find out how to do it by researching the particular subject that you seek. Not knowing how to do something is not an excuse not to investigate how; you can learn something new. Seek the knowledge that you need.

No one can stop you from acquiring the information that you want. Global information is easy to access through the Internet. In this new age of technology, the information can be accessed in a matter of seconds. Gone are the days where you had to spend days in the library scanning through books to find the information that you needed. Self-education is possible and easy. There are Internet courses that you can take that can give you flexibility, depending on the situation you are in. There is no excuse for not learning. If you prefer the old-fashioned way, there are still unlimited resources in the library, free for everyone to use.

You must want to acquire knowledge and become active in many ways to get it. If you want something, no one can stop you from getting it, except the limitations that you set for yourself within your mind. Find the right people who can help you. Do not be afraid to ask for help; you will be surprised by how many people are eager to share their expertise. Be very resourceful in your search for information. Keep on learning, keep on growing, keep on sowing.

Once you are able to acquire the information that you need in order to succeed, the actual application of knowledge is what will create the progress for you. It is not the amount of knowledge that you acquire that can propel you to succeed; it is how you use the knowledge in actual pursuit of the kind of life that you want. Potential knowledge is useless until it is used in an organized plan to guide your actions to create a positive change. This is why so many highly educated individuals are living from paycheck to paycheck.

Find a good use for the talents that you have. Your knowledge and talents are very powerful tools when used for the purpose of improving your life and the lives of the many people around you. If, for example, you have a talent for writing, make sure to develop it. One good way to start is to write in your diary daily. Aside from honing your writing skills, writing in your diary can be very therapeutic. You can also practice writing about topics you have passion for. Pick up books from the library to guide you. Better yet, buy the books that you think can be helpful for you so you can have them as reference anytime you need. Invest in yourself. Spend the time and money to enhance your mind. If you love to sing, take voice lessons, join a choir, or put a band together. Quality music is food for the soul. Music has the ability to uplift your mood. Do you have a passion for photography? What are you waiting for? Take some lessons or research on the Internet how to develop your ability to take pictures that tell stories.

Next, find ways that your passion can generate extra income for you in the future. Once you've honed your photography talent, submit your best pictures to magazines. You will never know your luck until you try it, not just once but as many times as you can until you succeed. If you like technology and computer science, take courses, learn what you can: it is a fast-moving industry in which you can earn a good income if you use your talent well. Do you have a talent for decorating? Start a business, create a very attractive brochure of your work, and get paid doing what you love. If you are curious about the human mind, learn about psychology and become an expert on the mind. Whatever interest you have, recognize it and develop it. Become the best in whatever you set your heart in. Compete with yourself, put your talent and knowledge to good use that you may further your growth and find ultimate happiness and satisfaction.

Merely having talent and knowledge is not enough to make a person successful. What makes a person successful is the tenacity of the actual *application* of the talent and knowledge possessed. Talent and knowledge that are not put to use remain only as potential. Potential is like ownership of a bar of gold kept in the safe (your mind). Taking the bar of gold out of the safe for the purpose of creating beautiful jewelry that you can wear or sell is putting your potential to use. Use your knowledge in focused, active motion for the fulfillment of your goals. Keeping your potential dormant will make it useless. Why did you take so much time to educate yourself when all you do is keep all you know in the confines of your memory? Pursue your dreams. Use your knowledge to guide you on a properly planned direction in the acquisition of your goals.

It is not enough to dream. Make daily steps, keeping your faith strong. Stay on track with utmost focus and soon enough you will find yourself living the life that you want. Life is an exciting journey full of lessons. You learn from your experiences and you learn from your mistakes. The information you acquire can give you strength. Strength can give you power. Power can give you energy and energy can make things happen. You have the ability to acquire all the wisdom that you want. Be open to learning. Read and learn from people before you. Learn from the instantaneous availability of information through the Internet.

Welcome the help of mentors, family, and colleagues. Learn to listen to suggestions and input from others. Positive guidance can help you. Do not be intimidated by criticism. Your humble open mind can help you acquire feedback. Feedback can help you pattern your next move accordingly. Pay special attention to constructive criticism, as this can improve your effectiveness in the future. Apply the knowledge you learn to the improvement of the quality of your life.

When I stand before God at the end of my
life, I would hope that I would not have a
single bit of talent left, and could say, "I
used everything you gave me."

—*Erma Bombeck*


Set your heart on your goal. Believe that it is possible. When your goal serves the greater good for a lot of people, it will generate interest and demand and ultimately bring you success. The positive forces of nature will rally behind you. Faith will strengthen your resolve and give you a massive push toward that foreseen future. Be a master of your own destiny. You are who you are today because of the experiences you had in the past and the choices you made that took you to where you are today. Your past has given you wisdom. However, today is what you have. Today you can have a fresh beginning. You can create the life that you want now. What you do in the present moment is vital to your success and happiness. Living in total awareness of the value of each moment will give you the courage to attain extraordinary things today and into your future.

I don't care how much power, brilliance or
energy you have, if you don't harness it and
focus it on a specific target and hold it there,
you're never going to accomplish as much as
your ability warrants.

—*Zig Ziglar*

## Learn for Life

Make it a point to learn something new from each day that comes. How much time do you use during the day in acquiring new knowledge that can help you? Are you reading materials that can increase your knowledge in your line of work? Do you read books that inspire and motivate your senses for personal, business, and spiritual growth? Spend at least a sacred hour each day for yourself, increasing your mental and spiritual growth. Early morning as you wake up is a good time for reading. Go to bed early and wake up one hour earlier than your usual time. As you wake up, your whole being is well rested, and your subconscious mind is more receptive.

At the end of each day, reflect on what you have learned. Have you added new information to your stock of knowledge? Make a detailed entry into your diary of any experiences that have given you enlightenment. Were there any challenging situations where you used your strong will to choose to see things from a better state of mind, bringing light where darkness had clouded the matter? Your will can create your own circumstances for you, making things happen by the angle that you choose to see the problem from.

If your line of work allows you to travel, use the time at airport gates and on the airplane to read. Alternate book reading with listening to audio books. Make sure to take notes on important things you have come across. Buy books that you feel will be good references for you in the future. Mark your book, use sticky notes, and underline phrases that seem to speak to you. You will gain deeper understanding with this habit.

Be a voracious reader. Reading stimulates the brain. It reenergizes the sleeping mass of brain cells. It records information for future use. Think of your brain as an in-house library, giving you access to information when you need it. Reading is a good way to pass the time. It is a limitless adventure that can take you to places you have never been before. It allows the mind to travel through time and space, using the written word to put color into the mind's imagination. Through learning the experiences of authors, you may refrain from making the same mistakes in the future. Reading increases your knowledge, making you more confident. It can inspire you, motivate you, and move you to that first action that can change your life to become more meaningful. It can help you learn to acquire true happiness and wealth. It improves your way of life.

The majority of people stop reading after graduating from college. Once in a while, they read the paper with all the dramatic chaos in it. Learning must be a continuous process throughout your lifetime. New information can keep the mind alert and young.

Listen to audio books while driving in your car. Driving this way can be more fun, like learning on the run. You can also use audio books as you exercise, shaping up your body as well as your mind. Buy educational books in line with your work to keep you abreast of new information. Underline phrases that catch your attention so that you can retain them better. Take notes for future reference; you will never know when you may need a particular piece of information. Retain information for the future. One day you may decide to write.

You can always look back into your notes and get ideas of your own that you can expand upon.

Invest time and money in seminars as well. Seminars on the area of your interest can reinvigorate you, giving you fresh energy and new up-to-date information. Information is power; use it to open up your world and reach greater heights beyond your imagination.

A lot of people spend money on cosmetics, clothes, gym memberships, and cars. Even if you care about how you look, make sure to take some of that money and invest it in your mind. Your mental growth and mental health is just as important as your outer physical appearance. Learning about the mind can make you understand yourself better. Understanding your thoughts and becoming conscious of the intentions behind your actions can make you become a more compassionate human being. Deeper understanding of the self can make you more tolerant of the imperfections of others, thereby improving your relationships.

Use your time effectively to learn something new in your area of interest everyday. If you are into sales, pick up books that can help you get the edge to become the best. Plan ways and strategies to increase your sales. Compete with your last month's best: commit to increase your sales by 20 percent first. Then on the second month commit to increase it by 30 percent. On the third month commit to increase it by 40 percent. The more up-to-date you are with information, the better you can handle the decision you have to make each day. You increase your value with the knowledge you acquire.

Continue to educate yourself, especially about things

that you fear most. Understanding the root of the fear can breakdown the hold of the imagined negative outcome. Learning elevates your capacity to enhance your state of life; growing widens your horizon to all sorts of possibilities; sowing what you have learned puts your knowledge into action. Action is what it takes to apply what you know and turn it into something that you can experience in the present. Harvesting what you have sown will reap you the success, happiness, and wealth that you have been searching for. The more you learn, the more you chip away the wall of fear. Eventually the remnants of fear will fall to the ground and record the imprints of the soles of your feet as you walk over them on your journey to discover a new freedom.

Education must be a part of your daily life if you want to accelerate to success. Remember, though, that knowledge is useless if not used to take action. You can have all the knowledge that you want—you can become a professional student—but without organized plan of action using your acquired knowledge, you will not improve your situation. Knowledge can guide you. It is like the ink that you can use to draw the map to your future. Like a soldier, you are equipped with enough ammunition to go onto the battlefield. However, without actually using your ammunition (knowledge) in an actual battle (application), you will not know how effective it is. Apply your knowledge with well-planned, organized actions to improve your life situation. Growth can only be experienced after practical action.

## FIND MENTORS

Learn from high achievers, as this will prevent you from making the same mistakes that they have, saving you time and money on your journey. Be in the company of people who are highly positive and motivated in life. Surround yourself with successful people who can inspire you. Two or more minds that think alike gathered together can become a powerful group. The blending of the positive forces supports such a group of people in achieving success. The bond they form becomes a pillar that the group depends on, especially when anyone among them needs assistance in any problem.

Together the group can tackle any problem from different angles through shared knowledge, ideas, and connections. These are people who can help you see that success is just around the corner. Creating mutual rapport with like-minded people can increase the velocity of your learning process. It is highly energizing to be surrounded by people who share your interests, views, and goals, and the shared emotions of the group can be very contagious.

## WHO DO YOU ADMIRE MOST?

Think of a person you admire. Why do you look up to this person? What qualities of this person do you think made him or her exceptional to you? Are these qualities and habits something that you can aspire to have? Are the achievements of this person a great example of what you want to aspire for in your life? Do you intend to work on imitating the good habits of this respectable person and coin them as part of who you are?

When a person of great influence captures your heart, investigate how you can emulate the qualities that made this person stand out among all others for you. Learn to follow in the footsteps of this person. Read about his or her accomplishments. If this person is someone you know, ask for advice. Ask him or her about the most dominating thought in his or her mind from awakening in the morning until bedtime. The answer can give you a picture of how this person thinks most often. The quality of thoughts within the domain of the mind is of vital importance, it drives a person destined for success.

A greatly successful person constantly thinks of progress, learning to improve everyday. A person who lives in a free country and yet is in poverty is trapped and overwhelmed by worries about the lack of resources. Dominating his or her mind are the miseries of debt, hunger, and fear. Feeling hopeless, their mind is stuck in this world of scarcity, constantly thinking of how bad the situation is, intensifying the severity of the situation. The difference lies in the quality of thoughts.

There is no good excuse for a person to suffer poverty, especially when this person lives in a free world. This earth is abundant in resources. There is enough for everyone to enjoy. It is for you to know exactly what you want and get it. If you want it bad enough, you will get what you want. Ask for what you want, expect that what you want will happen for you. Actions will spring out of your desire to change your environment to that which you want.

You have the power to improve yourself by studying the

examples of other people you admire most. Habits are acquired through repetition. Undesirable habits can be replaced. There is so much area to expand your horizon. Personal growth is for everyone who wants it. Improving what goes inside your mind improves the life you live in. The quality of your life depends on the quality of your thoughts. According to Daniel Goleman, author of *Social Intelligence*, "By mimicking what another person does or feels, mirror neurons create a shared sensibility, bringing the outside inside us." Surround yourself with success-driven people. The rougher the going gets, the faster they get up from a fall to move to the next available option. Their company will increase your ability to follow in their footsteps. Allow the positive exchange in a group of successful people to inspire you to mimic their successes. The energy of a group of people with a common drive can transform into well-directed positive movement that advances the whole group.

> Courage is resistance to fear, mastery of
> fear. . . . Except a creature be part coward, it
> is not a compliment to say it is brave.
> —*Mark Twain, Pudd'n Head Wilson's*
> *Calendar*, 1894

According to Nicholas Murray Butler, "Optimism is the foundation of courage." Optimism with knowledge can give you an edge. Action becomes imminent because of the build up of confidence. Knowledge takes away the fear, but knowledge alone will not take you to victory. That optimistic burning fire within you will produce determined actions that materialize amazing results by breaking through the boundaries of fear. Focus on the prize. Keep a continuous, productive action even when fearful. Fear will eventually diminish. Let that passionate fire take over your senses as you work toward your goal. Find a momentum. Your accomplishments will go beyond expectations.

# CHAPTER 26

## Share Your Knowledge and Wealth

One must spend time in gathering
knowledge to give it out richly.
—*Edward C. Steadman*

I wrote this book with the purpose of helping others to acquire success and happiness. I wanted to offer something that would ignite your ideas, lift up your hopes, and wake-up your desire to pursue dreams and transform them into goals. I wanted to impart ideas for happiness and success through my writings to inspire others, to give people a better understanding of how thoughts can influence reality. I want to become your cheerleader, cheering you on your way to the finish line.

There are many ways that you can share your knowledge to others. A good start is to mentor those closest to your heart: your children, friends and relatives. Become someone who enjoys inspiring people. Later on you can become a life coach. You can also write a book about your life or your field of expertise. I believe that every person's life carries lessons in it. They just need to be written down. Get that pen and start writing. Write in your journal. Make it a habit to write your ideas on paper. The information you accumulate can be used in your future book or future business. If you are verbally gifted, become a public speaker. You can teach and inspire people while at the same time getting paid for it.

To teach others about what you know is noble. Give a part of yourself. Sharing your knowledge deepens your own wisdom. Be the anchor of great inspiration. You are a walking example of success. People around you will question how you have reached this point in your life. Bring others up with you as you continue to climb higher grounds. There is so much joy in being able to lift other people up and encourage them to believe in themselves. Encourage your peers to view life with optimism, enthusiasm, and vigor. Spread the seed of fruitful living through positive thinking and strong faith. Be a mentor, excite others to find their inner potential to excel and become successful.

Do not look down on other people; everyone is human and must be treated with utmost respect and compassion. When you have more than what others have in terms of wealth and knowledge, make sure to use what you have to help uplift the lives of other people around you. Be open in sharing what you know. Sharing your knowledge can increase the depth of your wisdom. Become a mentor to someone; the gift of knowledge is priceless. Better yet, write a book about what you know and share it with millions of people. To touch one person can make you feel good; to touch many people all over the world with what you give is incredible. Or you can create a website that encourages people to learn and grow. Inspire others to achieve more and give more. Spread the message of peace and love so that fewer people may experience suffering.

Make it a goal to help others become happier in their lives. Make a flyer that inspires others in the field of your expertise, creating a difference where you can. Uplift others with your thoughtful kindness and loving actions. Then share a portion of your blessings with your favorite charities.

Find people with similar interests. If you are into writing, join a writer's guild near you. Get active in the group, make yourself useful. Connect with people who may be able to guide you as you guide them into the future.

If you are into public speaking, take public speaking courses. There are weekend courses that can be extremely helpful in honing your public speaking skills, such as the Marsha Martin Power Speaking Course or classes at Dale Carnegie. You can also check out the Toastmasters in your area, a group that meets every month to improve the public speaking abilities of its members. Volunteer to speak to kids in school for free in the beginning to get some practice and confidence. Later on, as you become better, you can start charging for your public speaking appearances. Even schools have a budget to pay for good speakers to come in to motivate the kids in school. Then join the National Association of Public Speakers.

Whatever your interest, do not suppress it, or ignore it. Do not fail to cultivate the hunger within you. Join a group of people who can inspire you as you inspire them to develop each other's talents. People with similar passions increase each other's enthusiasm, thereby increasing the group's creative common energy.

## WHY TEACH ABOUT POSITIVE THINKING?

There is a need to get the ground ready before you plant the seed. Stress the importance of the human thoughts to bring about the fruition of the vision. The power of the decisions we make in choosing the quality of our thoughts and the visions we entertain in our mind affects our environment. We are co-creators of our own future thanks to the thoughts we choose to occupy our mind.

# CHAPTER 27

## *Self-Confidence*

Confidence can make a big difference. Belief in oneself builds one's confidence. No matter what you do, when you are sure of yourself, you can easily win others. Like anything, confidence is something you can learn. When unsure about yourself, say repeatedly, "I can do it." Create your own affirmation, any words that can give you a positive boost to your personal confidence.

I was only 10 years old when we moved to Cebu City after my parents separated. I was entering 4th grade, and it was enrollment time, so I reminded my mother that she needed to go with me to enroll me at school. My mother told me, "You are big enough, go to the school and enroll yourself. I will give you the money, you need to figure it out yourself." I said, "Why can you not go with me? I do not know how to do it, I am afraid to go by myself." My mother replied, "If you do not learn to do it now, when are you ever going to learn? Besides I have a lot to do in the store." My mother was running our small store. I felt so neglected. I felt that my mom did not care about me. With resentment I went to school, walking thirty minutes under the harsh heat of the sun with a sad look on my face. As I arrived I saw that there were long lines of parents with their children. I thought I might have been the only one alone without my mother. I did not know what to do but I started asking questions from the people around me about how to get started. Once I learned where to go first and what forms to fill up and where to pay the bill, I became more confident that this was not as hard as I thought it would be. I succeeded on my first experience of the enrollment process. I believe now that my mother was teaching me to become self-reliant. She wanted me to learn to become independent. I thank her for teaching me early enough.

Do you feel good about yourself? Are you confident enough about the unique talents and skills you possess to face life bravely? Do you know where to find the information that you need to help reinforce your ideas so they become a reality? Do you feel that your earthly existence is useful to the betterment and enhancement of this world?

Confidence grows from acceptance and love for oneself. It is a recognition of being a co-creator of possibilities in a free world that allows for growth for the one who so aspires.

## DO YOU TAKE PRIDE IN YOUR PERSONAL APPEARANCE?

Are you dressed for success? Do you wear clothes that make you look presentable? Do you take time to groom yourself? How you carry and present yourself conveys a message to the people around you. It is an unspoken confidence. Taking good care of your physical appearance increases your overall confidence when dealing with people. Walk with your back erect and your head up, keeping eye contact. Conduct yourself with grace, not arrogance.

Do not look at a person fiercely, as to seem to stare; use

eye contact for attentiveness and deeper understanding. Your eyes can speak a thousand words within a moment. Be sure to use your eyes as the outlet of the positive energy from within you. When shaking someone's hand, be firm, with full attention, showing openness. A lame handshake shows disinterest and weakness in character. Walk with an aura of poise, grace, and elegance.

Success-driven people exude utmost confidence. They walk and talk with prime purpose. If you are seeking success, groom yourself for success. Act and walk with a purposeful stride. If you have to, fake it in the beginning until you become so good at it that the acting ceases. As with anything, habits can be learned. Success is imminent for a person who is determined.

My sister Susan, who teaches in North Carolina, relates to me a story about one of her students, Adam is a cute little boy in her first grade class. He was smaller compared to the other kids in class but definitely not frail. He would usually sit there pretending to listen but never participating. He wrote, but the writing was barely legible. It took Susan a while to get to know Adam, since her attention was mostly taken up by a couple of disruptive students.

Fridays were spelling test day. On the fourth spelling test, Adam caught Susan's attention as she realized he'd gotten his fourth zero. The next day, when she returned the papers, she called him to her desk. She noticed that when she called his name, Adam looked fearful. Then he had a quick gathering of courage. It was a fast transition. She told Adam to study and to please never get a zero again. It was a serious talk between student and teacher. Adam may have been scared inside, but he showed almost an adult-like confidence in the way he looked at her. Adam got the message. He promised to study and to try harder. From then on, true to his word, Adam never failed any spelling test again. The conversation Susan had with Adam made a big difference. She thought he would never make it to second grade, reports that she is happy to say she was wrong.

During the first grading period Adam's grades were failing in most of his subjects. Susan followed up on her conversation with Adam with a conference with his parents. They were very supportive and were like cheerleaders for Adam. His father was a German immigrant who works as a truck driver and his mother was a clerical worker. Adam struggled through the second grading period, but with some improvement. Two days later after the second period's grades were sent home, Susan approached Adam and asked him about what his parents said about his grades. He told her innocently and with utmost confidence that his dad said that they were better than before. Susan laughed and gave Adam a very big hug.

After this event, Adam became unstoppable. He started improving in leaps and bounds. Susan said, "I admire him and the loving support of his parents that gave this young child the confidence and assurance that he needed to move on and do the best that he could. Adam's parents were not critical and judgmental. They were there for him."

## HOW CONFIDENT ARE YOU?

Are you able to tolerate discouraging influence that clouds your confidence? Are you easily affected by other people's comments about you? Do you find yourself worrying about what people think about you? If you are constantly worried about what people think or say about you, you are simply wasting your time. For all you know, people are too busy to even be thinking about you. What people are thinking about is unimportant. Everyone is entitled to an opinion. An opinion is just an opinion; it does not change who you are. Conduct yourself in a way that elevates your confidence. Believe in the special qualities that you have in your possession that makes you valuable. As long as you know in your heart that you have treated people with love, respect and kindness, you do not have to worry about what others think and say about you.

Are there certain people who are always discouraging you from your ideas and goals? Hanging around people who are negative will get you nowhere closer to your goal. Avoid people who are constantly negative; they can chip away your self-confidence.

Your goal is to succeed, and climbing up the ladder to your goal becomes mighty hard when somebody under you is tugging at the seams of your clothes. You can fall from the pressure. Falling down with the negative people can earn you a lot of pain and bruises. Energy is lost and failure is all that you get.

To succeed in life, choose who you associate with. Find people you can learn from. Pursue learning their good habits and their way of thinking. Positive people will increase your enthusiasm to achieve success, increasing your desire and making your confidence soar.

CHAPTER 28

## Choice of Words Is Important
## for Success and Happiness

### WORDS—THE LANGUAGE OF THE SOUL

Words can often define your character. Words that flow
from your thoughts out of your mouth give others a glimpse
of what is in your heart and in your mind. Thoughts that
occupy the mind predominantly often find their way into the
spoken words of the bearer of the thought. Positive thoughts
pave the way to positive, empowering words.

When thinking often of wonderful things that you can do
to improve your life, do you notice finding yourself talking
about your hopes and dreams more openly? By the same token,
the more you talk about what you want and what you dream
of, the more your thoughts become clear, helping to crystallize
the vision. It is important to keep the mental picture alive.

Negative thoughts pave the way to negative, draining words.
Negative words make your thoughts become more clouded
with doubts and fears. Fear stops you from movement forward.
Thoughts and words have a cyclic relationship: good thoughts
produce good words, positive affirmations intensify positive
thoughts, and stated convictions can turn into faith. Faith is
vital for success. Understanding the reciprocal relationship
between our thoughts and the words that we use can open

us to an awareness of using both the power of the mind and the power of spoken words in conjunction with each other to become effective at creating a better reality now. Develop a habit of using words that empower you and others around you. Use words that are positive, inspiring, and energizing.

Choose your words for success. Words are powerful tools for building up your self-esteem. Positive affirmations can help you become more confident as a person. Tell yourself every morning, "I look great, I am happy, I am confident, I am a winner." Or you can say, "I have health, wealth, success, and happiness." Create your own unique powerful affirmations. Do not hesitate to use words that describe what you want. By using the affirmations repeatedly, you draw positive energy toward you.

Words can help you build a better relationship with your family. They can attract new friends and open up possibilities. Becoming successful has a lot to do with building relationships. The better you get along with people, the more people trust you. When people trust you, you can easily have a big support system when you have ideas that you want to pursue.

My sister Susan tells a story about a friend she had worked with named Sharon. Sharon is a science teacher from the Philippines. She took a teaching job in America through the Culture Exchange Program. While teaching, Sharon met and married Matthew, a fellow teacher. However, there was a problem: Sharon's visa stipulated that she had to go back to the Philippines for two years to share her experience. The Philippine guidelines state that science and math teachers are needed in the Philippines, so Sharon had to go back home and stay for two years before she could apply for a working visa.

However, Sharon and Matthew did not want to be separated. I told them that this was a really tricky situation, but that nothing is impossible.

Sharon and Matthew are people of strong faith. I often hear Matthew say, "Everything will be all right. I can feel it." On the other hand Sharon would say, "We are in God's hands. May His will be done." Sharon applied for a waiver and an employment authorization. She took action and kept her hope and faith alive. Her petition got approved, and she is able to stay in the United States with her husband and work legally as well. She is waiting for her green card. Their strong faith and positive affirmations have kept them together.

## WORDS INFLUENCE EMOTION

Words can affect how you feel inside, and they also affect how others feel around you. Constant use of positive words can make you feel good. Words have vibrations that affect the person releasing them as well as the people receiving them. Positive words can make people feel good. Words can increase endorphins, giving the feeling of joy. Uplifting words make people feel joy.

However, if you choose to use negative words constantly in your life, your life will become as dull and as unappetizing as the words that you often use. We unconsciously send off energy through our aura. Negative words send off negative vibrations into the surroundings, making the people around sense the dark energy. Negative words attract negative energy. People wonder why so many things are going wrong around them. Negativity drains energy, bringing in sadness and depression. Words that you use often have a way of molding your personality. They become an affirmation of what you want to attract toward your being.

Words can influence your actions too. Positive, energizing words can make a person spring into active growth. Kind, affectionate words can make a person feel warm and compassionate toward others. Optimistic and enthusiastic words can make a person feel driven to action. Inspiring, promising words can make a person full of hope, drawing the positive forces of nature toward him or her. On the other hand, when a person uses words that hurt another human being, it compounds the problem. Angry, mad words can intensify the bad feelings inside, making them brew out of control. The outcome can be disastrous and regretful.

Instead, be conscious of the importance of using words that best go in line with the values you hold dear in your heart. Defuse anger at its infancy by not getting carried away by your emotions. Replace negative thoughts with a more compassionate understanding of the person who was making you angry. Do not hate the person. You may be upset about the result of this person's action or you can be upset about the situation that involves you and this person, but personally attacking the person with hateful words can make it worse. Let the other person know that you are not happy with the result of the action, but never personally attack the person verbally. You cannot gain any ground from hating another human being. You may disagree with the result of their action, but it helps to find out what motivated this person to act the way that he or she did. You do not know what is in his or her mind, what fears and insecurities have tainted his or her thoughts. Actions are products of the thought. Other people's actions and certain situations can upset us. Tone down the volume of how the words are delivered when in a conversation with someone whom you do not fully agree with. Keeping your emotions in check can save you energy and pain.

Using opinionated words of undue criticism for others is a reflection of your own very own insecurities. Do not judge others. Look into yourself first, are you perfect? No one is perfect; therefore you are not in a position to judge other people.

## HAVE YOU BEEN EMBARRASSED AFTER A CONVERSATION?

Have there been words you have regretted uttering? Words, when uttered, create vibrations. Delivery and tonality affects the energy of the vibrations delivered. Verbal vibrations, whether positive or negative, influence the people receiving them, as well as the environment. Spiteful and insulting words delivered with fierce tone and mockery can inject pain to another human being and influence their emotional state.

Earlier, I talked about how not to allow other people's negative words and attitudes affect you. If you stay on guard, your awareness can shield you from becoming a victim. When you know better, you stay away from people who can harm your peace, back away from useless gossips, and learn to walk away from angry, explosive situations. Keep yourself in the company of people who, like you, are looking for the good and are seeking happiness. Be with people who seek to make the best of each situation.

I discussed the power of words here so that you may become a constant source of inspiration to others. You can influence others with words in a way that can make them feel excited, loved, and comforted.

Even unspoken thoughts give out vibrations to people and the universe. Do you remember a time when you met someone for the very first time and you could feel the negative energy in the room even before words are spoken? Could it be that the vibrations from the thoughts of the other person were dominantly negative and their dense energy emanated through the entire room, making you uneasy? Thought vibrations can affect the density of the atmosphere within the room. This is not scientifically proven yet, but one day the sophistication of science will find a way to measure the effect of one's thoughts on one's environment.

Do you find satisfaction in becoming offensive in your conversations with others? Offensive statements done to cause pain and insult can injure the soul of another human being. Sending negative vibrations toward people you are dealing with forms negative karmas. What you give out comes back to you. If you are searching for success and happiness, you need to give out positive vibrations constantly into the universe. Giving positive energy out is an invitation for more positive things to happen into your life. You can only get what you give out. What you give out will come back to you in abundance.

Practice consideration for others by thinking before uttering your words. Words are expressions of your inner thoughts. Make your dominating thoughts be of love and compassion for others. A wholesome mind is the foundation of a wholesome character. Your actions are the product of the quality of your thoughts. Help uplift the suffering of others by your kind thoughts. Your thoughts are the seed of your future actions. Your actions can affect those around you and the environment that you live in.

The good news is, we all have the ability to choose the words we use in our daily lives. This awareness can help in the practice of consciously choosing words that improve our inner feelings, thereby sending positive vibrations into the universe around us, opening ourselves to attract positive energy and positive possibilities in return. Words, when chosen well, can give a person power to lead, power to perform with excellence, and power to develop strength. Words are what we use to convey our inner self into the world. Choose words carefully, and choose words that empower you and the people around you. Positive words mold happiness, creating a breeding ground for success.

Examples of negative, draining words:
    Ignorant
    Stupid
    Hate
    Revenge
    Envy
    Jealousy
    Blame
    Idiot
    Lazy

Examples of optimistic, empowering words:
Love
Beauty
Awesome
Praise
Power
Happy
Kind
Rich
Abundance
Opportunity

# CHAPTER 29

## Focus on Your Victories, Not Your Failures

Trials are the steps on the ladder that leads to success. Each step brings you closer to your goal. Envision the victorious end, as you climb, crush the trials by the sole of your feet.

When you experience failure, do you spend time feeling sorry for yourself, getting discouraged, and feeling like giving up? Do you take the time to take a closer look to analyze why you failed? If you have failed once, you have not failed enough to make it to the top. Success is acquired after you have failed hundreds of times. Success is not a one-shot game. Do not be too upset the first few times that you fail. Practice, practice, practice with undying perseverance. Every shot becomes more precise than the last one. Success is a game played consistently by someone who perseveres through hundreds of off shots until the skill is formed. Without perseverance, success can only be a mere wish.

There is a lesson to be learned from each failure that can open your mind to fresh ideas and new angles that you can use to achieve your desired result. Be glad that in the process you have learned something new. Let each failure strengthen your resolve to keep on going.

There is a price to pay for success. If you have it in your heart, invest the time, effort, and passion to get to where you want to be. Giving up is not an option. Pushing through with will and determination is the key to eventually get to the finish line. An attitude of perseverance and a burning desire behind every action can make your vision of success come to life. Each failure takes you closer to your goal.

All of us at some point in our lives have experienced pain and failure. It is a part of life. Can you imagine how boring life would be if there were no challenges and obstacles at all? Life would be dull. Trials are practical lessons that mold your character.

I, for example, grew up in the Philippines. My childhood was a constant cycle of hardships. My parents fought a lot verbally, and at times physically. I remember crying a lot. It was a painful time in my life. There were times when we did not have much to eat. Luckily we had some plants in the backyard. We ate bananas and vegetables that we were able to harvest. After my parents separated we lived in a very tiny store that also served as our residence. After dark, we boarded up the windows. We had to put chairs up to make space for the straw mat that we slept on nights. We owned a one-burner stove at the far corner, under the stairs of the house above us. When we cooked we had to make sure not to hit our heads because the ceiling was slanted so low. Still, I look back at times and realize that my very hard past made me a stronger person. I am a survivor. I remember one day when I was about eight years old, I made a promise to myself: "When I grow up I will have a very peaceful home life." To this day I uphold that promise. I strive to radiate love and peace, as well as hope, around me.

## LEARNING FROM MISTAKES

Mistakes can serve as teachers. Learning from mistakes develops in you an arduous desire to overcome challenges along the way to your goal. Look at each mistake as a pebble of sand that can mix into the cement forming the foundation of the path on which you walk. The more pebbles of mistakes you accumulate, the stronger the path you are walking on becomes. Overcoming mistakes one after another brings you closer to victory. Victory is most glorious after the long trying road behind. Bathed in the electrifying victory, you become ready for yet more victories to come. When the mind translates its great potential into action, creative capacity flows like a river. Ideas begin to emerge easily as though you have become one with the current that drives the water to move.

Look beyond the struggles. Learn from them to gain strength. When you tumble, do not mull over your sorrow for too long. It can only intensify the pain. Instead of healing your wound, you deepen the cut. Stop focusing on your mistakes or any past sad history. Think more of success, and eventually success will find its way to you. Thinking about success more often attracts opportunities to your doorstep like metal to a magnet. It becomes easier to acquire success when your mind is constantly inviting it. Look at the present moment. Consider it a fresh start to do your best, one step at a time.

Focusing on your mistakes too much is an assurance of creating more mistakes in the future. Thinking of the past repeatedly will create that sad atmosphere in your life. You get what you expect. Why waste your time and effort? It can only hold you back. To move forward you need to get over the past and focus on now. Lack of awareness of the power of your thoughts can diminish your ability in acquiring success and happiness.

If you want to invite someone to a party, do you want to know who this person is? Is this person pleasant? Can this person add life to the party? Or is this person the unhappy sulky neighbor who can take life out of the fun of the party? Similarly, examine who or what you want to invite into your life. Do you want to invite success or do you want to invite failure? The thoughts that you have in your mind are open invitations to the kind of life that you want.

## WHAT HAPPENS WHEN A PERSON USES A MISTAKE AS AN EXCUSE TO QUIT?

Quitting blocks the flow of creativity, closing the door to any chance of success. Halting the current in its tracks stagnates the river, making the water stale. And unpleasant odor of decay permeates the water. When a mind has stopped trying to improve its present state, it starts to die, a cell at a time. The dream slowly dies with it. A person who quits and does not continue to pursue growth has allowed himself or herself to live life only through a cascade of unreliable circumstances.

## CONSCIOUS AWARENESS

Conscious awareness of the faculties of the human mind can help you live a life of true purpose. Become the navigator of the current of your life. Life's challenges must be looked upon as stepping-stones. Mistakes are teachers that exercise the mind and bring it even greater consciousness of its unlimited power. Discover the power within you that can change the way you look at your daily activities. When you have this awareness, each activity becomes an intrinsic ingredient of the growth of your mind as well as your spirit. A web of learned consciousness intensifies your sensitivity in resolving future challenges.

Your thinking mind must be aware of its artistic, creative capacity to feed your subconscious mind. Inject positive pictures in your thoughts. The subconscious mind will take any information at its face value. It does not know right from wrong. It stores the information you feed it as if it is what you want. It is essential to be aware of your ability to create new victories by the thoughts you entertain in your mind.

Get over the sadness in your history if there is any. Those past pains and failures are behind you now. Learn from them, but do not think about them over and over unless you want your subconscious mind to work against what you truly want. What you truly want is to succeed and find true happiness. Let your mind entertain positive thoughts and positive material that can provide helpful information to invigorate your subconscious.

## WAKE UP LIKE A WINNER AND THINK LIKE A WINNER

Remember that each day contains small successes. Each problem solved is a victory in itself. Each small victory brings you closer to bigger success in the future. Focusing on your victories, no matter how small they are, solidifies the faith you have in yourself. You will become a force to reckon with. Your winner instincts will take over when a situation becomes challenging. Winning and succeeding will become second nature to you. Your mind will be so strong. You will become a fire of unstoppable force, constantly energized by your ability to resolve problems. Your mind will see beyond the complexities at hand. The faith that you have in yourself will grow to overcome all boundaries.

Winners and successful people have a very firm belief in their abilities. Focus on your victories. Be excited about your now, the life that you have at this moment. Be aware of your ability to improve your environment. According to Maria Edgeworth, "There is no moment like the present. The man who will not execute his resolutions when they are fresh upon him can have no hope from them afterwards: they will be dissipated, lost and perish in the hurry and scurry of the world, or sunk in the slough of indolence."

My mother had a heart-to-heart talk with me and my brother when I was 10 years old and my brother was 13, and her words stuck with me: "I want both of you to have a good education. We will work together no matter how hard it may be, but you will finish school no matter what. My dream is to see both of you graduate college." We did not have any money, but I never doubted for a moment, I would finish school. In my heart I wanted to please my mother. I knew that it was important for her to see us succeed. My mother's words were like fire that continued to burn in my heart until I saw that her dreams would come true. We worked very hard in those early childhood and teenage years. Life was hectic when I was a full-time student and working in my mother's small deli and eventually going into the sewing business when I was sixteen. Looking back, I feel victorious, triumphant that I could make my mother happy to see her dream come true. I focused on winning no matter what. I did not see the hardships as obstacles, they were just part of the process, like a path I had to walk along to get to where I wanted to go.

A winner wakes up with a vision. It is important to start your day with the mindset of a winner. How you view the day ahead will make your day a better day if you choose to. Develop the events that you want to happen ahead in your mind's eye. Imagine the day to be productive and fun. Project the images of just how you want the events to unfold. Hold that vision for a few moments as you wake up, going through it and feeling the emotions that you may feel. You will in fact experience a day better than what you have expected. Positive thoughts and visions will transform your day as you want it.

The opposite happens to an individual who worries constantly even from the night before, tossing and turning, thinking about problems, getting frustrated endlessly. When the morning finally arrives, this person's thoughts are again consumed by doubts and worries.

Stop tormenting yourself with problems. Worrying constantly will not make the problem go away. Start your day wisely, begin with a good vision, and then hold that vision with faith. Tell yourself each morning, with conviction, "Today is a great day. It is great to be alive!" Repeat as many times as you want until you feel the emotions that you would feel when looking forward to something good. Make your greeting for the day with your own words. Use positive words that you may have a positive start, and you will begin the day ready for what lies ahead. You will have created more space for creativity in finding solutions to challenges that come your way.

Being a winner is fun. To a winner, problems become welcome activities that sharpen their ability to create solutions. This lifetime is a series of tests, and the faster you solve the problems, the better your status in life will be. A sharp mind with a positive vision is like a sharp sword ready to go to battle at any time. Like a warrior you are equipped with what you need to win the challenges of life. Live life to the fullest. Celebrate each small victory. Cherish the glory of each triumphant victory.

How to Focus on Victories:

Live fully in each moment.

Let go of past pain and failure.

Find strength in each triumph.

Have faith.

# CHAPTER 30

## Hope for the Best

Hope is a flicker of light in the dark. It is a glimpse of your desire that gives you a feeling of being so close to something that entices your heart. Hope makes you look forward to each moment because each moment holds in it a promise for the betterment of your life. It is a knowing that what you have longed for is sure to come, giving you energy to pursue the unknown. The hidden world presents a playground of surprises for the one full of hope. Treasure the hope within your heart and mind; it is through hope that your process down the road to success becomes more enjoyable and rewarding.

### WHAT HAPPENS WHEN A PERSON BECOMES HOPELESS AND CONFUSED?

A person feeling hopeless and confused has temporarily lost the grip of purpose. Hopelessness is felt when, internally, a person feels drained of meaning, as if he or she had fallen into a bottomless well, spiraling in confusion.

Take for example the loss of a job. A great feeling of emptiness is experienced immediately after losing a job one has held for a long time. Some people stay in the same job for ten, twenty, or even thirty years. Losing that reason to get up each morning and years of attachment to the same routine activity can be hard to get used to. If the loss is involuntary, starting a new line of work can be difficult in the later years. On the other hand, if the person was due to retire, not working can be interpreted as a new freedom to do a lot of fun things like traveling or picking up a new hobby.

Remember that your human assets of intelligence and creativity are not lost because of the change in your situation. Your talents are very much alive, for no one can take them away from you. Be aware of the wholeness of the self. It is time to search for something new with this awareness. Your self is independent from your work of the past. Your talents are intact; use them in your search for something meaningful to do, whether you are searching for a new career or finding something fun to do that captivates your senses in your retirement. Value your talents without prejudice. Keep using the gifts that you have to give yourself more confidence.

How can a person face the loss of freedom of mobility due to accident or aging? It is hard to comprehend the deep frustrations of someone immobilized because of an accident or due to old age. Speculating can be disrespectful to the one enduring this situation.

In the midst of pain, however, there is a hidden value that the naked eye does not see. The spirit dwelling within an injured body is very much alive and full of consciousness. In fact, the consciousness of an individual in this situation can delve deeper. There is ample time for reflection. Subtle joys can be multiplied within the confines of the soul, expanding the world beyond what is experienced physically. The mind is free to experience bliss no matter what the situation is as long as it is intact (no damage from an accident or not suffering from dementia) and is able to choose the kind of thoughts that dwell in it.

A good example is Christopher Reeve. He was a very successful actor and director, made famous by portraying Superman in the movies. He can be described as a great athlete with a zest for life. In May 1995, Christopher Reeve became paralyzed from his neck down after being thrown off the back of his horse during a riding accident in a competition. He was confined to a wheelchair and a breathing machine. It was hard for all to see Superman in this situation. For any average man, this situation might have been too much to bear.

However, Reeve rose to the occasion. He did not allow his physical immobility to stop him from attaining a new passion for life. He brought attention to stem-cell research to help find cures for neurological disorders and injuries. He was intensely passionate about this cause, enduring travel all over the country to speak to thousands of people. He brought more awareness to the need for cures for spinal injuries. He devoted himself to raising millions of dollars for research. He created the Christopher Reeve Paralysis Foundation.

Christopher Reeve continued to work, even starring in a film. He last directed "The Brooke Ellison Story." He was a great example of courage and true dignity in a situation that could have sent others into total despair. He used his mind in maximum capacity to induce creativity and talent even when his body was confined to a chair. He died at the age of fifty-two.

Another great example of great hope and courage is Helen Keller. She was only two years old when she became ill with a fever that left her blind and deaf. At the age of seven she became good friends with Martha Washington, the daughter of the cook. They communicated using the sign language they created together. Growing up, she touched the lips of people who were conversing with each other, trying until she realized that the words were related to things. Anne Sullivan, also visually impaired, became a teacher of Helen Keller. Helen Keller learned to speak by touching the lips and throats of other people as they spoke. She also learned Braille, and she used it to read many different languages, such as German, Greek, Italian, and French.

Helen Keller did not allow her disability to limit her capacity to develop the talents that she had. She was the first deaf and blind person to get a college degree. She became an author and she was very passionate as an activist for the blind. She had overcome adversity by not dwelling in self-pity. She focused on her strengths, rising above her disability and using her will to go beyond what others expected of her. She learned to speak the language of the people who have complete sight and hearing. She made what seemed to be impossible attainable.

Despair is created in the mind. It is a state of mind. Just like happiness, it is a choice. No matter what your situation is in life, remember to create a stable state of mind that can carry you through into a better place, a state of mind based on gratitude for what gifts you have. Count your blessings. Have hope in your heart. Write down all the things you are grateful for. If you are unable to write them down, ask someone to write them down for you. Read the list of your blessings every morning to remind you of how much you have. Focus on your blessings, not your misery, and hope will emerge out of the darkness.

# CHAPTER 31

## Inspiring a Winning Attitude

> If you don't like something change it; if you
> can't change it, change the way you think
> about it.
>
> —*Mary Engelbreit*

Attitude is how you respond to people and situations. How you respond to things can help you become either happier or more miserable. The course of your life depends on the attitude you choose to have. Whatever it is that you are presently experiencing, nothing is ever permanent. Things can change for the better. Dwelling on something that momentarily upsets you can cause you to lose peace. Losing peace can make you unhappy. You do want to be happy. It is natural for a human being to want happiness. I aspire to be happy because I want to enjoy life. Most people know what they want, but a lot of us need guidance on how to acquire it. The key is in the attitude. How can you use that positive inspiring attitude to add to your happiness and the happiness of others around you?

A good situation combined with an awesome attitude can escalate into great new beginnings. Your confidence expands with your healthy attitude and opportunities become endless. A bad situation combined with a good attitude from you can be improved. A bad situation paired up with a bad attitude can be a recipe for unhappiness, pain and disaster. Happiness is an attitude.

> We either make ourselves miserable and
> weak, or happy or strong. The amount of
> work is the same.
>
> —*Francesca Reigler*

Actions inspired by your positive attitude and true determination and passion can make you a winner. Make it an obsession never to give up. Giving up is not an option to a person destined to win. A winner keeps going no matter how tough it gets. Focusing on the goal and pursuing it with full enthusiasm is the key. The winner sees the obstacles along the way as stepping-stones to the dream. Your faith, passion, and creative action will unfold your dream to become a reality.

## KEEPING A GOOD ATTITUDE IN HARD TIMES

As a child, I hung around my brother Sunny a lot. We would climb trees for fun, play hide and seek, and collect and play with multicolored marbles with other kids in the neighborhood. There was no television or video games to occupy our time. Our creativity came into to play. We were given chores to do by our parents even at a very young age. I learned to wash clothes by hand. I washed clothes almost the entire day on Saturdays. I would sit on a small stool at the back of the house. It may not seem to be a fun thing to do, but I got used to it. I realized it was my job assignment at home. I washed for the entire family. The mountain of clothes looked tremendous after a week. I would take them all to the back of the house in huge baskets, separating the whites from the colored ones.

As I started to work, I would start to sing as well. I love singing. I like to think I may be a singer in another lifetime. I sang songs of Barbara Streisand, Whitney Houston and other American and Filipino artists. I pity the neighbors that had to listen to me every Saturday. Hopefully they had earplugs. Singing for me made the day go by smoothly. Music made my heart feel warm, making work less tedious. After washing, I would hang the clothes on the clotheslines beside the house, securing them with clips so the wind would not blow them around the neighborhood. I remember soaking the whites with laundry detergent, squeezing lemon on them, and leaving them under the sun for a few hours to make them brighter. Heavy jeans that mostly belonged to my brother were a different story: I had to stomp my feet on them many times or hit them with a wooden paddle, otherwise my hands and wrists would become too raw. I used to have red inner wrists when I went to school on Mondays anyway.

Sunday was the ironing day. Inside the tiny deli where we used to also live in, I would open up the ironing board, which occupied half of the space of the store area. Outside the store, I would work on igniting the charcoal in my heavy metal iron. Once the coal was hot flickering red, I carefully ironed our clothes, making sure that no flying sparks landed into the material and constantly checking that the iron was not too hot to make contact with the various kinds of materials of the clothes. That metal iron was heavy. I would sweat ad sweat and it took hours to finish the job. My hands were hardened with calluses from years of ironing clothes with that old fashioned metal iron. Afterwards I would reward myself with a nice big muffin from our merchandise at the deli. Oh, did I savor that taste after a hard day's work as a young girl!

I was already in college when my brother got out of the seminary and joined me and my mom in the basement apartment. We moved out of the store just as I was about to enter college. When it came to food, my brother was king. It was his assignment to walk to the wet market every so often to buy the necessary food for the family. We loved getting our food fresh. Sunny loved to cook. While my brother cooked, I got myself busy cleaning the house. I was the one who waxed and scrubbed the floor. We had a concrete floor in our basement apartment but a fly could practically slide on it. I would go hands and knees to meticulously apply wax all over. I would wait for a few minutes and then scrub it with a coconut husk. We called it "lampaso." It is a coconut with its husk and shell completely cut in half. The shell inside is chipped off around the edges to prevent it from hitting the floor while scrubbing. I used my bare foot to push it against the floor in a sliding motion forward and backward movement until I had thoroughly scrubbed the whole place. The shine it gave was awesome. Doing this in 80 to 90 degrees heat made me very sweaty. We did not have air conditioning or even fans. But I did not mind. I loved keeping our home clean. No matter how difficult the situation, a good attitude is key to make life easy.

Music is a great part of the Filipino culture. My father used to sing a lot around the house. He had the most brilliant voice. He sang English songs and Spanish songs. Sunny played the guitar. I tried to learn it as well, but did not get that far. But I loved singing and music. We grew up singing and dancing in family gatherings and parties. I was sent to Hawaiian school dancing, where I learned to move my hips to the drums of the Tahitian music. It was fun. Now in America, most Filipino families that I know own a karaoke machine. Parties are hilarious. Even if a person is a bit out of tune, they sing just for the fun of it.

To have fun and be light hearted like this when you are living under trying conditions may sound hard to comprehend. It is the attitude that one chooses that makes life a little better. We were happy even when we did not own much. A person's ability to perceive things in a better light can make a difference in making him or her happy.

I have lived in America for 19 years. The standard of living in the States is one hundred times better than what I experienced back in the Philippines. There are opportunities that can be taken. Make sure to take the necessary action to use these opportunities to improve your life. Use a winning positive attitude in each moment so that you may succeed in getting what you want.

## DO PEOPLE ENJOY BEING AROUND YOU?

A pleasing personality is magnetic. Your personality is a reflection of the inner energy stored in your being. A happy, upbeat person has a higher positive energy stored within the mind and body. What a pleasure it is to be with someone who can be a source of so much fun and energy. This type of person lights up a room, bringing life to the party. Positive vibrations coming from this type of personality permeate the atmosphere of a room, creating a soothing comfort.

How people react to you is a mirror reflecting your character. Do you conduct yourself in a way that shows respect and concern for others? Does your physical and facial expressions convey openness? Do you use proper eye contact to connect well in conversations? Do you listen to understand deeper? Or are you too busy trying to say what pleases you without allowing others time to share?

## THE VALUE OF LISTENING

Understand yourself that you may gain understanding of another. Listen to the voice within you. Everyone longs to be heard and accepted. We need to connect with others, we want to have meaningful relationships. First learn to listen. It takes much discipline to simply listen. When you listen with full attention, you focus your complete self toward the person you are communicating with so that an emotional link may start to take place. Look into the eyes of the person to intently absorb the message of the exchange. Relax and listen without interrupting. Your patience and attention can open up a bridge to true comprehension. Many people are too eager and too excited to speak their mind. They talk so much about themselves or about the subject being discussed that in the process they lose the true benefit of communication.

Communication is a two-way street that can generate enlightenment for the people involved only if they give some time to listen. Interruptions break the flow of the message being conveyed. Communication can only be effective when both parties have successfully linked. A good conversationalist has mastered the art of listening. Listening with the true intention of understanding makes the other person feel important, special, and heard. Your total attention makes the other person feel at ease. The atmosphere becomes more relaxed, tensions dissipate, and each individual can come up with the right questions to ask to obtain a deeper understanding of the other person or the matter discussed. Trust starts to build, and both parties open up to a better understanding of each other. Your eager willingness to understand another human being reflects your selflessness.

Start to build trust from the infancy of any relationship. Trust is galvanized and tested through trying moments over a considerable length of time. It is therefore earned. Trust between two individuals is powerful. It can be the beginning of a great partnership. Earning trust builds a good foundation in a relationship. Each trust-earning event strengthens the structure of the foundation you are building. Be a person of your word. Promise only that which you can deliver. Uphold your honor by being true to your word and intention. Hear what others have to say by listening. Listening can give you deeper understanding. Being understood is a basic craving of man, who needs acceptance. Acceptance brings joy, love, and happiness.

## USE LISTENING AS A TOOL FOR UNDERSTANDING, NOT AS A SPONGE FOR INTERNALIZING NEGATIVITIES

Do you feel drawn too much to the problems of others? Do you feel obligated to internalize the problems of others to show sympathy? Do you feel an obligation to listen to, and some satisfaction in feeling, other people's painful emotions? Internalizing the emotions of other people around you is like allowing yourself to become a human vacuum cleaner, accumulating pain. Taking in pain is taking in the negative energy. Listening to too much negativity can affect your very own state of mind. Recognizing the problem without internalizing it can give you ample positive space in your mind to work on creative solutions that you can suggest. Detachment is useful in situations where rational thinking is needed to acquire solutions.

Are conversations that dominate your days mostly about endless problems and complaints? How do you feel after each of these types of conversation? Do you feel drained after using so much of your time absorbing the troubles of others into your consciousness? Worrying too much with others can create a feast of dancing negative impulses among the people concerned that can darken their mood and compound their negative feelings. By doing this, you are wasting valuable time that you could have used for growth.

Encourage positive discussions of possibilities. If there is a particular problem, suggest an idea or action to be taken to resolve it. Ask the recipient of the problem how he or she may resolve the problem. Influence others with your positive mind; be the hope that lightens up the group. Become a catalyst for positive conversations, bringing life and energy to any situation. To become a positive influence with others, you need to become a good listener. Listen not just with your ears, but with your heart as well. Pay attention with total interest in the one who is speaking. A person who listens will win the heart of many people. Listening with understanding connects two or more minds to a harmonious mingling.

Every human being desires to be understood; when you give of your time to listen, the other person will appreciate your true concern. You are allowing the other person free expression without so much interference. You are not just there to talk about yourself and your achievements; you are there for this individual and this person will forever be grateful for your attentiveness and possibly your future friendship. The rush of the modern society has given us less time to breathe and be able to communicate with a deeper degree with other people. Take time to know a person by better listening.

When you are at a party, do you feel comfortable, moving around the room with confidence, or do you find yourself in a corner with your arms across your chest just not knowing what to do next? Prepare yourself mentally before going to a party. Imagine yourself smiling and moving around the room with utmost confidence. Imagine meeting very interesting people that can add to your circle of friends. Enter the room as if you own the place; imagine being in your own living room, be yourself, and smile. Thoughts that you have in your mind translate into the physical manifestations of either confidence or awkwardness. It is all up to you to pick the confidence-building thoughts instead of dwelling in your fears, looking too shy to connect.

Be aware of your physical and facial expressions. Smile sincerely, hug warmly, shake hands firmly, do things wholeheartedly. Whatever you do, make sure that you are expressing a positive physical expression of what is in your mind. If your mind is filled with negative thoughts of criticism and defeat, your facial expressions as well as your bodily movements will show the distress that you are experiencing within. When shaking the hand of someone while entertaining the thought of how ugly the person's necktie is, you become distracted, by the negative thought about the tie, and your handshake might become lame and cold, your facial expression might show a slight distaste of that vision. Learn to see the person beyond the tie, keeping your enthusiasm for the meeting with undivided attention using eye contact and a firm handshake. Sincerity can be felt in even a short meeting; never neglect to be considerate, even with the thoughts that you have for another individual.

A warm, sincere smile can light up the room. Happiness radiates throughout the atmosphere where a person giving such a smile stands. How easy it is to give a priceless gift with that sweet smile, yet not too many are eager to give it. Give a lot of gifts everyday with your ready smile; it is heart warming and will not cost you anything. A smile can bring you more happiness, because when you give love through a smile many times a day you will be the recipient of so much love in return.

If you really want people to like being around you, practice all of the above plus add sincere love, respect, and compassion for all mankind. Do not forget to spice up the atmosphere wherever you stand with enthusiasm for life. Enthusiasm is electric. It is a contagious, upbeat state of mind that brings so much life to a gathering. An individual with well-tempered enthusiasm bears gratitude for the gift of life.

## DISTANCE YOURSELF FROM NEGATIVE PERSONALITIES

There are people who can bring a cloud of gloom to a gathering. Have you met someone who seemed to love misery? This type of person dwells on everything that went wrong throughout the day. In fact, this type of person can recount the dissatisfactions of life going back to day one of their unhappy awareness with a sad, sulky face that translates stored pain and sorrow, which are negative energies. Extremely irritable, angry people have accumulated a lot of negative energy. Like a leech, they suck the blood out of anything fun. They have a love affair with misery. The more they talk about their discontent with life, the gloomier the atmosphere becomes wherever they are. Gloom is embedded with their every cell. They have planted the seed of unhappiness many times. Complaining compounds the gravity of their sad situation. What they harvest is more unhappiness. Being around this type of person is draining.

Avoid hanging around gloomy personalities, lest they muddle your mind. Being around people who constantly give out negative energy can influence how you feel, and can influence your outlook in life. Soon enough you will find yourself spiraling into dissatisfaction with life. This cycle is an endless, tiresome journey heading toward failure. Complaining personalities do not have a definite purpose in life. If they had one, they would be busy pursuing their purpose instead of wasting so much time cultivating a lonesome disposition.

If you happen to have a strong positive energy, try to help gloomy people see the light. Show them the fun that awaits enthusiastic people. They need to be ready for a change. If you feel someone you know is seeking happiness and satisfaction, then at least it opens up the path for change to take place. But if you know in your heart that it is a challenge to you, avoid the negative personalities. Choose to be with people with positive attitude toward life.

## USE YOUR MIND AND BODY AS STORAGE FOR POSITIVE ENERGY

Hold a positive vision in your mind. Fill every cell in your body with positive energy through a positive mental attitude. What you store in your body radiates into your personality. If you want to have an upbeat personality, provide your mind the positive input it needs to transform you. Think of thoughts as food for the mind: the more healthy thoughts of love, happiness, and abundance you have, the more you will experience fulfillment in life and the more magnetic your personality becomes.

Not only will you enjoy a transformation of your outer personality, positive thoughts can give you a better life. Picture the most wholesome lifestyle that suits you. Think of how wonderful it will be to live in the house that you want. Imagine the red convertible that you want to drive. Dream of that perfect job that gives you ample time off to spend with your family while generating triple the income that you presently earn. You might be able to pick up a new hobby with the additional time and resources, or they may enable you to go fishing with your kids or increase the number of times that you play golf with your friends. Does this seem too perfect to be true? It is possible to live close to perfection. First, believe that you as a winner deserve only the best. You have to know exactly what you want and believe that you deserve the best.

What is the difference between you and someone successful? If someone has done it before, there is no reason why you cannot do it. Not just do it, but to do it even better. Infuse an inspiring winning attitude in all areas of your life. Go for what you want with utmost vigor. Your winning inspiring attitude will draw people toward you. You will start creating the right connections. Become a winner through your positive attitude and grace.

Why is it important to listen?
> Listening can give you understanding.
> Listening allows you to connect with others.
> Listening builds a foundation of trust.

A person with an inspiring winning attitude has:
> Positive outlook
> Strong faith
> Inspired action

# CHAPTER 32

## *Conquer Procrastination*

Have you been meaning to organize your closet, clean up the garage or your basement and never seem to get to complete it? That happens to most of us. We keep putting it off and putting it off, and we have only ourselves to blame when the scenery makes us miserable.

I have wanted to write this book for a long time. I would write several pages at a time, but was not able to consistently stick to it. I started many times but was unable to keep on going. The fire seemed to die too quickly. There were many things that preoccupied my attention during the day and during the night. Twenty-four hours was not enough to do what I needed to get done. I made a lot of excuses for not working on my book.

Then one day, I made a commitment with myself to go for it 100 percent. I figured that if I wanted to write a book, I had to keep on writing until I am done. I told myself, "I will not stop. I will put the time in and pay the price for what I want." No one could write the book for me other than myself. I lived in my pajamas when I was home for months. I blocked out the noise around me; at other times I locked myself in the basement. At nights I was able to write a lot when everyone was asleep. I had the whole kitchen to myself. I loved thinking while sipping my tea, writing my ideas while I enjoyed the peace in my kitchen. I would stay up until three or four o'clock in the morning. Needless to say I had to apologize to my whole family for neglecting them. But they were very supportive of this work and are excited to see it happen.

Recognizing the value of each present moment as if it is all that you have will allow you to use your time effectively to pursue your goal of success and happiness. Procrastination is the result of indecision. Inability to make a decision has kept many people in the same status in life for many years. If you are content with what you have, then that is a decision that you make for yourself. As long as you are happy, that is all that matters. However, most people would like to elevate their way of life. It is human nature to want more, to aspire to something better, to have a chance to improve what is on your plate.

There is a price, though, to attain any kind of progress. Are you willing to pay the price for change? Are you willing to sit down and take time to create an idea to get to where you want to be? Are you willing to draw a well- defined plan to execute your ideas? Then, are you willing make a decisive action to make your plan come to life? Will you unleash from within you the undying persistence to pursue the completion of your goal? The decision is for you to make.

## FORM GOOD HABITS TO COUNTER PROCRASTINATION

Each human being is unique. One person can have a series of good habits and some bad habits. Some people may have more bad habits than others. There are habits of others that may annoy you and there are habits that you have that get in the way of your success, like procrastination. Habits are formed from repeated exercise of the same action through a period of time. The good news is that a habit is not a part of the core of the person. A bad habit can be changed and replaced by a good habit.

Awareness of the process is needed to negate the old habit. When this awareness is achieved, the process of introducing the new positive habit in place of the bad one can become more effective. Consistency is the key to overcome falling back to the old habit. There is no strict time frame of exactly how long the process takes. It may vary from person to person. Create a good habit by conscious repeated action, which eventually takes on a life of its own. The habit becomes automatic; it does not take the kind of effort it did when you started to create it.

A person seeking success and happiness like yourself needs to coin good habits for life to achieve your goals. Examples of good habits to form include: (1) positive thinking, (2) getting things done, (3) good communication, (4) being true to your word, and (5) compassion for others.

Now is the right time to seek success and happiness. There is no perfect time other than now to find your way to improve your present situation and turn it into the kind of life that you want. Economic ups and downs have nothing to do with whether you succeed or not. A lot of people use the trends of time as an excuse for inaction. There are many opportunities available no matter what type of economic situation the country is in. A mind seeking to succeed will find opportunities no matter where and no matter when. Your success depends on your ability to capture ideas, make a visible written plan on how to make it come to life, and then take action steps.

Do not be afraid to ask for help. You will be surprised at how much you can do with assistance and good reliable advice from people you trust. If one person refuses to help you, ask another and keep on asking until you find the help that you need. Never be afraid to ask. Ask people for something out of the ordinary each day. Pretty soon you will get rid of the fear. Many doors will start to open for you when you are able to ask for what you want and what you need. Finding resources is a quest for a person seeking to succeed. If you let your shyness overwhelm you, the journey to success will be too slow. Learn to conquer your fear.

Make a decision to get started now. Today make a promise to yourself to start doing something about what you need to accomplish. If you have been planning to clean up the basement and get rid of unnecessary things, resolve to get started. As soon as you get started, it becomes easier to keep going. It also helps when you commit yourself to getting it done. If you want to write a book, sit down and write down your possible book titles, then make an outline of your chapter topics, and get started. If you want to lose some weight, start exercising today, eat better, drink a lot of water, and get enough rest. Do not wait for tomorrow to start what you can do now. Postponing work is unproductive. If you want to succeed in becoming a person of action, keep on moving with purpose. Do not procrastinate. Procrastination can only give you unhappy regrets.

Procrastination prolongs the agony of reaching any desired

end. It drags any task or project into uncertainty, possibly losing you deals and opportunities along the way. Precious time is lost. Time is as precious as gold. When time is not used wisely, success stays on the back burner. Procrastination can make you lose the momentum. You need momentum and constancy of motion if your goal is to succeed in life. Unfinished work can make you lose confidence in yourself and make you lose credibility with your employer or customers as well.

## COMMIT TO TAKE IT TO THE FINISH LINE

Do you take pride in finishing something that you have started? Do you remember what a great feeling of relief you experience after finishing a task? Finishing something of good value to you gives you a lot of pleasure. Finishing something of so much importance can give you a euphoric high, as if you had just finished a climb to the top of a huge mountain. Accomplishments add to your sense of self worth, giving you an even greater incentive to strive for more. That feeling of being on top of the world makes you feel like you can do more. It gives you a sense of pride and confidence that there is more where that positive energy came from.

Or do you find yourself starting too many projects without finishing them? How does that make you feel? Do you feel frustrated with yourself for all the unfinished work? Do you find yourself making too many excuses not to do the work? Organize your thoughts and make some written plans for your daily goals so that you may accomplish more. Focus your mind and energy on the task at hand. Use undivided attention while taking action steps. Use total concentration to get the work done well and in a timely manner.

Discipline your mind to take responsibility squarely head on, conditioning your physical self to act according to the demands of the work at hand. When the mind is ready, the body is ready to do what the mind commands. When the mind is timid and weak, the body becomes as timid as the mind. Nothing can get done when the mind is asleep. Wake your mind up with a vision of the finish line. What do you see ahead of you? Think of the wholesome feeling of fulfillment. Make a commitment to keep doing instead of simply talking and procrastinating. Verbalizing what you want to do is good at getting you excited to get started, but remember that it is action that can make things happen. No one gets to succeed by barking at the moon.

Procrastination is the enemy of the person who wants to succeed in life. Make a point of completing work one project at a time to have complete undivided focus. Winners love the triumph of crossing the finish line. Commit to your goal. Keep the vision alive every step of the process. Take each step with passion. Celebrate with each small victory. Each of them will take you closer to the completion of the task or project.

## CREATE YOUR OWN TIME FRAME

Learn to conquer the urge of postponing work. Be a get-it-done kind of person. Finish work ahead of deadlines. Better yet, create your own time frame for each task, ahead of the true deadline, and stick with it. Commit to get it done before the deadline you gave yourself. To suppress procrastination, you need concentrated effort focused on your particular goal.

It is one way to eliminate distraction. Imagine yourself as a horse running in the race of life with blinkers. Your focus will be on the road ahead. Your commitment to win will be directed in the right direction. Do something toward the task at hand every day. Even if you do not get it done today, at least you have chipped away a portion of it, getting you a bit closer to the goal. Once you get started, it becomes easier to keep going. Be proud of your progress; it can energize you to keep moving on.

> Program your mind to overcome procrastination by continually visualizing your tasks as completed. Visualize your goals as already achieved.
> —*Brian Tracy*

Do not sink into timidity. Unfinished projects or work can overwhelm you, especially when new tasks are piled up on top of the other ones. It will be very difficult to get anything done. You will get confused figuring out where to start, let alone how to possibly finish.

## GET ORGANIZED

Keep your home neat. Give away anything you have in your closet that you have not used in the past two years. There is a big possibility you will never use it again. It will open up space for the new things that you buy. Throw out unnecessary things that are stored in your basement and garage. Give away stuff that can be useful to someone else, to the Salvation Army or another thrift shop. You can also sell things through eBay. Getting rid of things can give you breathing space.

Reduce the clutter in your workspace. File papers that are important, then toss all unimportant ones into the wastebasket. Throw out old magazines. There is no need to keep them. Old information can become obsolete after a while. After you have cleared out a lot of junk, you can feel good working in a clean space. Be on top of your responsibilities, then rejoice after each task is done.

## WRITE IT DOWN

Make a list each night of what you want to accomplish the next day. Number each item according to the degree of its importance. Put the hardest task on top of the list followed by the easier ones. The next morning, work from the top of the list, getting rid of the harder task. After that, the rest of the list will get done so easily. Cross out from the list what you have done. At the end of each day you will be very pleased and relieved to see how much you have accomplished. Anything left on the list can be carried over to your next to-do list in the evening.

Writing down your daily goals the night before is very effective. It helps store the written information into your subconscious mind. I practice this myself every day, and I amaze myself with how much I can accomplish. Preconditioning the mind to commit to working on those tasks the next day is a remarkable way to conquer procrastination. You become mentally ready to take action toward making things happen, getting things done so work will not pile up and aggravate you. You will feel fantastic and useful. At the same time, you will see things moving forward toward your long-term goals. Make sure that your daily list includes steps that bring you closer to your ultimate goals.

> Goals are dreams with deadlines.
> —*Diana Scharf Hunt*

I cannot reiterate to you enough about setting goals. Write down your long-.term goals, i.e. what you want to have happened in ten years. Write them down in present tense as if you have achieved them already. You can write as many goals as you want.

Examples of ten-year goal:

1. My relationship with my family and friends are as strong as ever, and they support me in all my endeavors.
2. I am healthy and strong. I exercise an hour each day. I eat healthy unprocessed food. I feel young and strong.
3. I am financially secure. I can retire when I choose to.
4. I own one hundred properties that are well run by a reputable management company, creating cash flow, earning equity, and giving me tax incentives.
5. I contribute a good portion of my income to my favorite charity, helping others improve their quality of life.
6. I own a house by the water with a very scenic view.
7. I own a red convertible Mercedes Benz.
8. I play golf, improving my vitality and at the same time

enlarging my social circle.

9. I have improved my communication skills. I speak to large groups of people often, sharing my principles to help others become successful.

Examples of five-year goals:

1. My relationships are strong. I am a good listener. I am selfless.
2. I have a great network of mentors guiding me.
3. I have multiple sets of income.
4. I have tripled my income. I am able to invest more so I can retire young.
5. I own fifty rental properties and I am buying more.

Examples of one-year goals:

1. My relationships are great due to my better attitude towards people and life itself.
2. I am intensely seeking multiple income possibilities. I am investing for financial security.
3. I have a network of mentors who are positive thinkers and success driven.
4. I am applying the secrets of success in all facets of my life.
5. I have multiplied my income, working less, and giving me time to seek other creative opportunities, allowing me to spend more time with my loved ones and pick up new hobbies.
6. I have paid off all my debts (credit card), freeing me more money to invest.
7. I live below my means so I can save and invest more.

Examples of daily goals:

1. Return phone call from a private investor for possible partnership on a commercial building.
2. Take the bank manager to lunch to discuss future real estate investments. Create a good rapport.
3. Place an ad in the paper to sell the property on 3 Harrison Drive.
4. Call the soup kitchen and make a plan for the family to volunteer to serve dinner to the less fortunate over the weekend.
5. Order flowers for Cindy's birthday.
6. Take the kids to karate school.
7. Have dinner with the family.

These are just examples. Create your own goals. Search within yourself and ask, "What do I really want?" Write your goals in present tense as if you are experiencing them at the moment. Put all the details into writing. The written notes will help you to visualize your goal better, creating a more concrete picture in your mind. Your clear vision can enhance the faster realization of your dreams.

Each time you are able to finish a task or project ahead of deadline, make sure to reward yourself. Go for small rewards like a good cup of coffee. Better yet, get a massage. You can also play ball with the kids in the backyard. Now that you have finished work early, you have extra time to do more fun things with the people you love.

Let the good feeling sink in to give you enthusiasm to start working on new projects. As you lie in bed at night, your mind is set on tomorrow's activities. Things will flow better when planned ahead. Relax as you drift to sleep. Picture yourself in a blissful state of fulfillment. Feel the glory of winning run through your veins. Go through the triumphant emotions. Feel the euphoria as though you have already arrived at your true destiny of success.

Get rid of procrastination by:
- Setting goals
- Getting organized
- Finishing work ahead of deadlines
- Rewarding yourself

# CHAPTER 33

## *Workplace Strategies for Success-Driven Individuals*

There are eight key lessons to succeeding in the workplace:

1. Share your vision. In any size organization you will need to convince those at all levels about your vision. This can be a very challenging process. The strength of your belief can make your vision happen.

2. Develop goals at work. Once you have defined them, constantly evaluate your goals in light of ever-changing directions from others at more senior levels. Flexibility is key in this fast-changing world we live in. If you are not flexible then you can break.

3. Get the work done and create your own deadline ahead of the true deadline. This way you will be ahead of the game. Create your own time frame. Encourage others who may not be as driven and set out deadlines for them. Some individuals are very good followers, so your approach is the key to help them find the fire.

4. Delegate work and ensure that your team has the necessary tools and resources to accomplish the objectives you have given them.

5. Make decisions, as success can only be accomplished through countless decisions. This will be key in achieving

advancement, due to the progressive changes that timely decisions bring. Be decisive and encourage input from all team members. A well-calculated risk approach will be needed.

6. Monitor progress. Even if you do not accomplish all your goals as quickly as you would like, you will still need to create progress daily. Progress can be in the form of a follow-up phone call or communication of changes that may affect the goal. It may be as simple as an upbeat reminder, "Please let me know if you have any questions on the ABC project."

7. Overcome setbacks and obstacles. A success-driven individual precisely communicates his or her ideas to his supporting team and at the same time openly welcomes feedback from them, allowing them to attack the problem more effectively as a powerful group.

8. Be flexible and open to changes as you may be required to change directions and shift resources off project A to project B. Decisive decisions and follow-through are the key to adapting to the ever-changing face of the work environment.

## COMMITMENT AND RESPONSIBILITY FOR YOUR CAREER

If you thirst for appreciation at work, do more than what is expected of you. Volunteer to be given more responsibilities, then get the work done ahead of time. Arrive at work earlier than others and leave later. Make it a point to work all the hours when you are at work; never waste your time on useless activities while getting paid. Companies lose a lot of money due to many workers who do not value time. Many workers use their time in gossiping and surfing the Internet. Make sure that you are productive with each moment that you are paid for. Get away from useless gossips. People will respect your commitment to your work and responsibilities.

Dare to be different: be there physically and mentally for your company, be willing to do what it takes to increase your positive contribution. Soon enough your concentration will bear creative results. Your superiors will start to notice you. If your company does not notice you, someone from another company will. Opportunities will open up for you in many ways. A great percentage of employees are only willing to do what they are paid for. Most complain about anything extra they have to do. Come five o'clock in the afternoon, they are in a hurry to get out of work, rushing out of the building. These employees look like someone is chasing them out scared. That is the attitude of a perishable worker. People of this caliber are not creating value for themselves or the company. Companies tend to like people who are truly there. Give more of yourself, so that opportunities will be endless for you.

How much time do you work each day? How much time during the day do you waste? Do you understand the main purpose of why you were hired to do the kind of work that you do? Are you devoting your work hours to important, effective actions with measurable outcomes? Are you maximizing your time at work in fulfilling the purpose of your position?

Examine the activities that you participate in from the time you get into the office until the time that you leave. Are you doing too many unimportant activities? Are you wasting your time? Do you spend a lot of time socializing with coworkers? Learn to break free from small talk without being rude. People will respect you for your work ethic. Anything that takes your time away from the more important things that can elevate your performance level is a waste of your time. Recognize the tasks that can have profound effect on your bottom line. Can the activity add to your value? Can it enhance your productivity? What you need to do first are the things of vital importance that can create growth and increased income for your company and yourself. Small tasks that are not of vital importance can be done later or can be delegated to other people who can do them well. Your effective performance, due to your dedication, will shine. People will know that you mean business.

Activities you are involved in during the day can either increase your value or decrease your value. Weigh your actions: the less effective you are at using your time for actual profitable actions, the less effective you are as a worker. Without properly managing yourself and managing your time, you will stay at a mediocre level in your company. Prosperity will look like to be a far distance. If you want to excel in your line of work, focus on using your time for effective actions. Give more than what is expected of you. Compete with yourself. Strive to volunteer to do more work, then finish the work ahead of time. Give your best-quality work, and soon enough people at a higher level will notice your excellent gifts. More responsibilities will be assigned to you, giving you more ways to show your talents. Doors of opportunities will open up for you in form of promotion or higher pay. Other companies will hear about you and want your services as well. Words can get around and the next thing you know, your world has changed for the better.

If you find yourself making too many mistakes at work, you may need to reexamine your situation. Do you love your occupation? Do you come to work looking forward to getting things done? Do you feel a sense of accomplishment after each working day is over? Are you able to use your creativity to address the challenges that you encounter? Are you unhappy about your work ? Then it may be time for you to assess whether you stay in this profession or not. Unhappiness is often projected into a lack of the concentration needed to get things done the right way. Work must satisfy your self-worth by giving you a sense of pride in each challenge you are able to overcome. Loving what you do increases your creativity and happiness.

Remember that you are not stuck. If you continue to work for the sake of having an income to pay the bills and to take care of your family, you are hindering your possible expansion in another field that may allow you to grow and feel satisfaction. Living from paycheck to paycheck is like a rat race. You tend to go in circles, chasing your tail, eventually getting dizzy and exhausted from the run.

Some people are employed in high-paying positions but are unhappy for various reasons. The educational system in our country does not prepare the young for the true reality of what they will one day face in the financial world. What ends up happening is that well-educated Mr. Jones lands a very high-paying job in the six digits range after graduating from college, and becomes overwhelmed by the enormous income that he is receiving. Excited by the new freedom that the fresh income gives him, he decides to get married to Mrs. Jones and have two beautiful babies. He then buys a huge house with a pool in the back. He goes on to buy a top-of-the-line sports car aside from the family SUV that he already owns. Before he knows it, he is living from paycheck to paycheck. Stress can bite hard in the corporate world. There's no need to add this kind of financial burden on top of it. It becomes a nerve-racking-cycle.

If you are unhappy about your job, try to find out what you can do to give you more satisfaction. Focus on your strengths to become more productive. Are you worried about the risks involved in changing your career? If you decide to stay because your job pays well and provides a good way to support your family and your needs and you simply cannot take a chance, change your attitude toward the job. Changing your attitude will change how you feel inside. How you feel inside affects your creative abilities, making you more productive. Learn to love what you do or it will drive you insane. Either you decide to find something better to do that will make you happy or decide to adjust your attitude to ease your mind.

If you are a highly paid corporate man living in the rat race, break the cycle. Change your ways. Cut down unnecessary expenses, live below your means so that you may have some money set aside to invest in other ventures. In this generation, we all need to plan for our own retirement or we will end up working until we are seventy-five years old. Having multiple sets of income is a good way to ensure that if you lose your job, you will still have other income coming in from the various investments that you have cultivated along the sidelines. Put money away in your company's 401(k), invest in real estate wisely, invest wisely on some stocks, and buy and sell goods through the Internet. Being totally dependent on one income without any other sources makes a person vulnerable.

## ARE YOU HAPPY WITH THE WORK THAT YOU DO?

Do you find yourself inspired as you wake up to get ready for work? Do you greet the day with a new hope for what it can bring you? Do you feel good as you enter your work space? Does your work increase your creativity? Do you feel that you are able to develop your talents through your line of work? Do you feel challenged enough? Are you growing and learning? Reflect within to assess the amount of satisfaction that your work provides for you.

So many people complain about their unhappiness with their work. They do not get paid enough for what they do. They don't like their boss. Work is so stressful. Work is not challenging. Blah blah blah blah blah. It goes on and on.

After listening to some people complain about their jobs, I sometimes think they are trying to convince me that they are shackled into their position helplessly, mercilessly by force. Whatever happened to the freedom of the democratic world? Has everyone forgotten that this is a free country? This is a country that allows you to have a choice. No one is forced to stay at any given position. However, some people have stayed in the same job for ten or twenty years. Why complain about it now? Do something about it instead of complaining about the situation. You are responsible for your own happiness.

You have chosen the job that employs you, you have chosen to stay even after you realized that you are not paid enough, not challenged enough. Remember that you are totally free to expand your horizon and seek another job that can rock your world. Do not be afraid to become fearless. There are so many opportunities out there, if only you investigate, so many ways to uplift your skills through education. You can even take classes through the Internet. Sharpen your skills to arm you for bigger dreams.

Work must satisfy your soul. If the main purpose of work is only to get a paycheck to pay the bills, work becomes an annoying task. Work must be something you love to do. It must be enjoyable, challenging, and fun. Peace of mind can be achieved only when you are happy doing what you enjoy most. What you do for a living starts from a choice that you made. You are not stuck in your line of work. You have a choice to change your situation by acquiring more knowledge in a field that you want to enter. Search for other possible employment that you think will give you the most satisfaction.

You can also explore ideas to start a business on the side, while you keep your present job a little longer to help finance a new business. Banks will lend you money when they know you have a steady income to make your monthly payments. Let us say that you are thinking of starting a business. OK, start one now. Do not expect wishes to come true if all you do is wish. What is needed is a detailed plan regarding what business it is that you want to start.

Extensive research can be done on the feasibility of the business idea. Ask for the assistance of people who have expertise in the area. Find the right people who can help you materialize this plan. Once you have found the selected group of trusted people, unveil your plan and let them know that you consider each of them as a team player. You have just created the mastermind group. A mastermind group is a group of people who have a common goal and interest with you. All members spend time brainstorming on ideas and they help each other solve problems. Allow the expertise of each individual to contribute to the business. Create a concrete business plan together. Then find financing by laying out your business plan to the bankers who will listen. Do not feel disheartened when one or two banks turn you down. Keep on trying, knock on every door until you find someone who can see value in your plan. As soon as you get financing, go for it in full active faith. Implement the plan with well-guided, determined actions. Make your dreams come true. Actions can make things happen, so keep on doing and keep on moving.

As the business grows, you can choose to go on your own full time. One good thing about owning a business is that the harder you work, the more money actually pours into your own bank account. Working with others can make the business owners and stockholders richer as you work harder. Becoming your own boss can give you a sense of pride, freedom, and accomplishment.

Make it a point to have multiple ways of creating a flow of cash into your bank account. Read books on investing, real estate, and stocks. Read from the experts and ask the advice of experts before making your very own final decision. Do not totally rely on others when it comes to money. Know the facts, analyze, and then follow your instincts. It feels good to have total control of your own destiny.

# PART 5

# Moving Forward to Sucess

# CHAPTER 34

# Take Responsibility for Your Own Actions and Your Own Life

We are responsible for the choices that we make. There is freedom in taking control of our own destiny. You are where you are because of the choices that brought you to this point in your life.

Your success is not dependent on others. Success is your prime responsibility. Success is dependent on your commitment to a progressive vision. If you want to succeed, you need to have success consciousness occupy your mind. Your dominant thoughts throughout the day must be of abundance. Thinking of the hardships in life and constant worrying will increase your poverty consciousness. It will bring about negative domineering thoughts in the mind. Your thoughts become a part of your belief system, whether good or bad. Belief attracts that which you think of most often. Nature will then grant you what you most desire. The quality of thoughts entertained within the conscious part of the mind is recorded into the subconscious mind. The subconscious mind serves as a sponge, soaking in the information at its face value; it does not judge whether the information is good or bad. Therefore, it is up to you to use self-discipline to take total control of the thoughts that you allow to dominate in your head.

Thoughts are like food that you provide for your mind. Healthy thoughts of abundance will create that reality for you. Unhealthy, impoverished thoughts will bring about ill, impoverished realities for you. The defensiveness of human nature is an easy escape. It is much easier to blame others when things go wrong instead of looking inside. Ask yourself questions like, "Where did I go wrong? What actions must I take to repair the problem?" Denial of truth and a chosen blindness to one's responsibility is very common. When people experience downfall, they blame their sad childhood, their unsupportive husband or wife, the moon and stars rather than themselves.

The truth of the matter is that you are responsible for the things that happen in your life, whether directly or indirectly. Your decisions and actions bring you to wherever you allow yourself to be. You are in the situation you are in because of the choices you have made. No one forced you to be here. If you happen to have tragedies that occurred in the past, bury them in the past. What is important is that you still have today to flourish and be the best that you can be, no matter what experiences have injured you in the past. Challenge your life to be lived in the moment because no matter what you do it is all that you have. If you do not give value to your present moment, you are either living in the past or just watching your life pass you by. Living in the NOW, in total consciousness can improve your tomorrows. Let the past give you strength to push forward. Do not let the past hold you back.

A person does not just all of a sudden go bankrupt because his or her partner likes extravagant shopping sprees. The fact is this person allowed his or her partner to continually drain his or her resources without confronting him or her. A mutual discussion of finances must take place early in a relationship so that each individual will take responsibility for keeping the family's finances in a healthy state.

Live below your means. Acquire debts that are considered good debts, like real estate and business capital debts that can create a cash flow for you. Avoid credit card debts: they can drain you when they get out of hand. High-interest-rate debt that does not generate income is unwise. When buying a car, buy a slightly used car to save money. A brand new car freshly driven out of the parking lot of the dealer loses $3,000 of its original value instantaneously. Be also wise when buying a home. Buy a home to live in, not a home for a showcase for excessive extravagance. Living below your means is being responsible financially. Make sure to have money deducted automatically for your company's 401(k) especially if the company matches it. You can also set up a Roth IRA, which has more flexibility. Saving money before getting taxed is like paying yourself ahead before paying Uncle Sam. Also put money away in a savings account. Make sure that you have enough for all your living expenses for at least one year if you were to lose your job.

Living way above your means can put you in too much debt. Credit card debts with high interest rates can drain you. Homes that look grand have huge taxes and need expensive furnishings in them. Fancy cars have high monthly payments, high insurance, and expensive upkeep. After paying all your bills, do you have anymore left to use for other investments?

Do you have enough money to sustain you and your family for at least a year if you lose your job today?

Have you lost any money in an investment? If you seek true success, you would have invested some time and money in some venture. Some you win, some you lose. If you have lost at some point, please get over it. Excessive mourning over your loss will not make the money come back into your pocket or all of a sudden reappear in your bank account.

Be confident with your abilities, your talent and knowledge are your best assets. Add a great personality into your package and you become a dynamic individual. Any money that you have earned and lost can be earned back again. Once you have been able to experience success prior to losing money in some investment, you will be able to find your way back. Just like riding a bicycle, even if you did not ride the bike for a year, sitting on the bike again and riding it becomes automatic. You do not have to relearn how to ride, you know exactly what to do. The vehicle becomes a part of you. Success is very similar: once you have reached the top before, no matter how many times you have failed and lost, climbing back to the top becomes second nature to you.

Donald Trump has succeeded many times and has failed many times, even to the extent of declaring bankruptcy. He is always able to rise again because he has built a strong brand name for himself, and his name is able to withstand the many downfalls that he has to get through. His name connotes class, success, and finesse. He uses his people skills to overcome his adversities by communicating to the bankers and being frank about his situation. He is a great example of a man of true mental strength and determination. As a young man, he used to walk in Manhattan and dream of one day owning the most luxurious high-rise buildings in the city of New York. His thought became his reality.

So, if you have lost money before, never give up. You need focused confidence with fired-up, determined action to acquire new wealth for yourself. You are standing in the midst of massive opportunities. Start digging where you are instead of looking somewhere else. No matter where you are, as long as you live in a free country, you can succeed. You are free to acquire what you want. You are not tied down with any hindering rules. What you think is more important than your location in the equation. Your thoughts can change your environment. If you know what you want, your thoughts will take you where you want to be.

First you need to know what you want to achieve in life. What is your primary purpose? Communication and information is a click away from your computer or from the library computer. Seek opportunities where you can find them. Apply for a job anywhere you want, and then relocate. Explore the new world that opens up in your journey. The quality of your thoughts is more important than the address and the condition of the neighborhood where you live in. Improve your thoughts and your life will improve. You will be able to take yourself to a better place where you desire to be with positive thoughts and strong determination.

Take, for example, an individual who complains about being married to a lazy, useless, jobless individual, proceeding to completely blame the unhappiness and discontent of their own situation to the other person. Blaming will not resolve the problem. First of all, nobody forced the couple to get married. Surely both accepted each other "through thick and thin until death do us part," per their marriage vows. Of course things change, however, there is always a choice to either stay married or not. If they choose to stay married, then the complaining partner can stop complaining and start looking at the good qualities of the other person and be someone who encourages, supports, and find ways to help the other person find enthusiasm in life.

If you are married, remember that you are still an individual who can create your own decisions, especially when it comes to personal growth and career. Hopefully you have picked a supportive partner who can motivate you with your goals in life. Instead of blaming others for your unhappiness and misery, look inside yourself and say, "I take full responsibility for everything that happens in my life." If you are not happy with your situation, ask yourself, "What decisions and actions can I take to change the situation to suit my needs?"

Remember that you are not stuck. You have the freedom to choose. You have the power to change your situation in life. If you are not happy, it is time to assess what you can do to make your life better. Take responsibility for everything that happens in your life. The awareness of the importance of your choices and actions can lead you be to a happier person.

# CHAPTER 35

*Materialize Your Ideas for Success*

Find hidden value in each feasible idea to unlock the door to success. An idea is like a pearl hidden in a shell in the middle of the ocean waiting to be harvested. When the pearl is found, it can be turned into great value. An idea can be a concept for a great invention. What all great inventors have in common is finding the idea in their mind first.

Great men and women of the past generations have been known to have the habit of writing and scribbling their ideas every so often. Carry a small notebook with you during the day. Write down any idea while it is still fresh: if you are unable to record the idea you may have just missed an opportunity. You can also carry a small digital audio recorder that you can speak to whenever the moment of need comes around. Speak to your audio recorder clearly, describing in detail what ideas come into your mind.

Learn to decipher ideas into possibilities. Toy around with an idea to determine how to make it happen. Countless trials and experiments eventually can materialize an idea into a concrete, tangible, usable product. It usually pays to have a plan, investing time and perseverance. In the end, persistence wins and a vast amount of people will enjoy the comfort and benefits provided by the new product as it becomes widely used. Success will follow.

> An idea not coupled with action will
> never get any bigger than the brain cell it
> occupied.
>
> *—Arnold H. Glasgow*

When an idea comes across your mind, jot it down immediately. If not captured, like a bubble it is lost. As if you had let a pearl slip away from your hand back into the ocean, the value is lost for you. The next person who discovers this idea will reap its rewards. You want to be the one to enjoy the fruition of your idea, because it was born first in your creative mind.

If at some point in your life you have allowed a pearl to slip away and lost opportunities, do not beat yourself up for it. Do not regret past opportunities; there will be more to find once you have mastered the use of your mind. You can create your own opportunities. Everywhere you look, opportunities start popping up. Your deeper inner awareness will guide you to find new opportunities where others do not see them. Worry not about the past opportunities you have missed; there are unlimited resources for the one who is aware.

Your very own mind is the key to unlocking great ideas for the future. Give the mind liberty to be creative with its abilities: use meditation to unravel the hidden treasures that reside within. The universal pool of knowledge can only be tapped within the peaceful, quiet confines of the soul. Use audio books to guide you, write down any ideas that come to you from your meditations. Take time to allow the growth of any idea in your mind. Let your imagination work the details.

Ponder the possibilities of it coming to life. Is it going to benefit a good number of people? Is it going to improve the way of life of the people you intend to serve? Is it unique? What steps do you have to take to be able to make it happen? Do you know some people who can help you to make it into reality? Are you willing to invest time and money? Are you willing to find financing for this project?

> Money never starts an idea. It is always the
> idea that starts the money.
> —*Owen Laughlin*

It does not take money to make money, it takes a great idea with a clear vision and an inspired plan. It takes intense desire peppered with perseverance. Use a detailed plan to guide your actions in making a great idea come to life. Ideas can become products and services for the future. Ideas can also be compared to seeds that you plant and fertilize to grow. Nurture your ideas, research their possibilities; discuss and brainstorm with trusted colleagues or friends about how to make them happen. Create a plan that gives you an overview of the step-by-step process of how to bring it to life. When ideas materialize to become a useful product or service it can improve the quality of your life and the lives of others around you and around the world.

> Discovery consists of seeing what
> everybody has seen and thinking what
> nobody has thought.
>
> —*Albert Szent-Gyorgyi*

Taking your ideas to fruition can bring you success, which will reward you, comfort you, and provide financial independence. Do not disregard the value of those quick thoughts that come and go. Capture them by quickly writing them down. Find the significance each idea can provide for you and the world. After seeing its viability and importance, decide to make it happen. The intensity of your intent will become the driving force giving you a push forward.

## MATERIALIZING SANTA CLAUS

When I was in kindergarten, around the month of November, all the children were looking forward to the class Christmas Party where were going to be exchanging gifts. Our teacher discussed the program with us and asked for volunteers to participate in it. A lot of hands went up. Some kids volunteered to sing, some wanted to dance, and another wanted to recite poetry. I raised my hand excitedly, and when my teacher called my name, I stood up and told the class that I wanted to be dressed as Santa on that day so I could distribute the gifts. Another girl said that she wanted to be Santa too. My teacher nodded, but I could feel that she did not take me seriously. At recess, I told anyone who would listen that I would have my mom make a Santa outfit for me to wear at the Christmas party.

As soon as I arrived home that day, I told my mother that I would be dressed as Santa Claus at the upcoming Christmas party and asked her to make the outfit for me. My mother asked, "Are you sure about this? Does your teacher know?" I assured my mom that the teacher knew. My mother went to the fabric store and bought a plain red material and some white material to use for the trimmings. She also bought a lot of cotton to make the beard. Mother meticulously made a Santa outfit.

December came along, and on the morning of the Christmas party, I got dressed in my red and white Santa outfit, complete with hat, belt, and a fake beard made of cotton that mom glued to a material attached to my ears with some elastic bands. I arrived in full regalia. As I entered the classroom, everyone's attention was on me. My teacher's eyes went wide open as though surprised, and then a bright smile came across her face. Looking back, I think she was amused. She ushered me next to the tree, announced that Santa Claus was here, and asked a photographer to take our picture. The program went smoothly. Santa had the pleasure of handing each gift to the class.

Later on my classmates said that my costume was awesome. Most of them said that they thought I was just kidding when I told them that I wanted to dress like Santa on the party. Well, I proved them all wrong. When my heart was set on an idea that I believed in, even when I was just six years old, I pursued to make it happen.

Your ideas can materialize when you focus on creating the situation to make it happen even when other people may not believe in you. No one can stop you if you want it bad enough. Take courage in believing that you can make your ideas come to life.

How can ideas bring success? Ideas can create:
Products
Services
Business
Comfort
Financial independence

# CHAPTER 36

## Moving Forward and Opening Up to Change

> They must often change, who would be
> constant in happiness or wisdom.
> —*Confucius*

A lot of people become very comfortable in the familiar routine of their lives. They fear that any drastic changes could disrupt the rhythm that they are used to. Some people complain of their lack of resources, but at the same time they are stuck on frozen ground. They are not doing anything to improve their situation.

The world is in constant motion; so must you. With the rapid changes throughout the world thanks to modern technology, if you do not keep up you can easily fall behind. Change is good for you. It can elevate your situation. It can introduce you to new discoveries. Be open to change, be in constant motion. Stopping can make the air stale; it stinks when you are stuck in stagnant water. You do not want to feel too comfortable with a meager, routine, boring lifestyle. Continue to be progressive. Treat each moment as a chance to grow, a chance to find new ways to improve yourself, your surroundings, and your relationships. The more open you are to change, the more opportunities you will find to pursue to make your situation better.

Move forward. Learn from the past, but do not keep on looking back. What is important is the present and what you can do now to move forward. Vividly imagine your objective. Feel as if you are living it now. Ask yourself, "What steps can I take to make it happen?" Write down the steps, and look at your list daily.

There is nothing more permanent in the world than change. Be flexible with life's changes. Be adventurous. Live as if this moment is all that you have. Do not be stuck in a routine. The fear of the unknown can hinder you from making that first step. Once you muster the courage to take a leap of faith, things will fall into place, and then fear will slowly diminish. Be brave. Do not be afraid to fail. Success cannot be achieved without practice. Failures are just that, an exercise you have to undertake to reach success. The more failure under your belt, the closer you are to the door of success. You emerge stronger after every fall. Courage is an asset, part of the character of a true winner. Having that inner strength makes you look forward to change.

> Success is to be measured not so much by
> the position that one has reached in life as by
> the obstacles which he has overcome.
> —*Booker T. Washington*

Learn about the route you are about to take extensively so you can calculate your risks. If you let your fear overcome you, it will be hard to win. Crush fear with knowledge. Eliminate fear by reaffirming to yourself that there is a key to every door. All you need to do is to find it. If you cannot find the key, be creative and find an ax to break the door and free yourself of fear.

A lot of people are afraid of change. Sometimes the door of opportunity is in front of them, but they are afraid to take the initiative to open it. There is an element of fear attached to the mystery that lies behind the door. Conquering fear involves mustering the courage to open the door that leads to opportunities. Opportunities can reward you with passage on the road to a better quality of life, a life that is rich in abundance. Abundance can only be achieved by the constancy of change. Change is always happening all around us. Fighting against it will drain you of energy. However, welcoming change increases your flexibility to handle greater challenges. A winner feeds on challenges like a bird feeds on seeds.

My brother Sunny came to America a few years before me. He got a job with the United States Navy. We were so proud of him. Having a family member in the US Navy was a very big deal for Filipino families. I can recall the day when I received the telegram from Sunny, who was at that time in Manila, saying that he had passed all the examinations and would soon be going for training in the United States. I was alone at home, but as I read the telegram I started jumping up and down with joy. I wanted to tell the world how happy I was. We did not own a telephone, so I ran out of the house to tell my neighbors and friends the great news. When my mother came home from church, we both danced with joy.

For a family to have a son or a brother in the United States Navy meant that the future is getting brighter. The family will benefit financially and have the chance to be able to come to America. The Navy sent a percentage of my brother's income automatically to my mother. It was a nice change for us. There was some cushion, money in the bank. We wrote my brother very long letters telling him about our lives back home and how much we missed him. In turn he wrote about his adventures all over he world. He sent us pictures of him in the ship with his friends and pictures of the different places that he went to. Sunny eventually settled in San Diego.

One day we received a picture of him posing in front of an orange used car. He looked proud, as this was his very first car ever. In his next letter he told us that he had to get rid of that car because the car would not reverse, it just kept going forward, so it became a dilemma when he needed to park. Oh how my mother and I laughed so hard. We must have turned red. A few weeks later another letter came containing a picture of a brand new red sports car. Wow, we looked at that picture for so long, trying to look at every angle of it.

At times Sunny became homesick in his letters. Mother and I kept writing encouraging positive letters of support to keep Sunny's spirit high. We had a small tight family. For my brother to leave the nest of the family was like going out of the comfort zone and to a new world. It was a drastic change of environment and culture. But it was a good one. My brother made some very good friends and he started feeling better. He came back home a few times to visit us and to visit his girlfriend Aissa. They eventually got married and have two handsome boys named Andre and Simon. Sunny made the Navy his lifetime career and has just retired.

Change is good. When there is change, something is moving and evolving. It is part of life. Learn to move forward and welcome change into your life.

## CHANGE IN YOUR WORK

If you are looking for a job, what you need to do first is reflect on what you want. What do you want to do that will best make you happy and satisfied? List the type of work that is in line with your interest. Are you qualified for this type of work? What can you do to improve your skills? Can you take a course to make you more attractive to the industry? Once you figure out what you want to do, research the companies that you are interested in. Check if these companies are hiring, know the products and services that each company offers. Check the Internet or visit the nearest library to practice answering possible interview questions. Use a yellow pad to write down your answers to all practice questions. Read your answers over and over until you know just what to say to any questions an interviewee will throw your way. Then put together a resume that best shows you as the right candidate for the position you are applying for. Limit your resume to two pages. After sending out your resume, make sure to follow up. Job-hunting must be looked at as a challenge. The better you have packaged yourself in your resume, the better your chances of getting called in for an interview. The more presentable and prepared you are at your interview, the better your chances of getting hired. The more applications you send out to outstanding companies, the more choices of employers you will have. It feels good to have several choices lined up.

According to Brian Tracy, "The most remarkable thing about your fears is that if you face them squarely, they diminish." Freedom from fear is very liberating. You will live life like a child, fearless, joyful, and full of energy. You will always be ready to learn how to undertake what lies ahead. Be curious, let your creativity flow. Change allows you to experience new things. New experiences can enhance you.

When things do not go the way that you want, change directions. Try another path, with a new plan. Consider the setbacks as bridges you have to cross to make it to your treasure island. Keep the burning fire within as you cross the bridges. Your desire and focus will eliminate your reluctance. Each step becomes an adventure in itself. Treat your goals as a fun challenging game that can be won over and over with prizes of unlimited value. The only limiting factor to winning the game is the imagined boundary in your mind that hinders you from getting what you want. Limiting thoughts such as insecurities and doubts block the mind from seeing the goal. Instead of seeing clearly, the mind is clouded, unable to see clearly the proper direction to take.

You get only what you ask for with persistent endeavor. The attitude that you have toward the exciting game of life can help you to discover new ways to play against all odds. Winning in life is a mind game. Believing that you are a winner brings you a few inches away from the finish line. Persistent action drives you through it. Partake in the invigorating game of life by what you put in your mind.

Learn about the path you are about to take to rid you of your fears. Knowledge eradicates fear and paves the way to the eventual fulfillment of your dreams. Your dreams have a way of finding you as you embrace change as a part of moving forward while you sail through life.

Opening up to change can make you have more:
Flexibility
Constancy of motion
Progressive action

# CHAPTER 37

## *Find Your Luck*

> Luck is what you have left over after you
> give 100 percent.
>
> —*Langston Coleman*

Do you believe in luck? You can make yourself lucky, though not in gaming tables or Lotto. You can create luck with your ability to recognize an opportunity, followed by actions to make it happen.

Luck can sometimes stare you in the face and yet you still do not see it. You do not see it because you did not search for it. You miss to notice luck's presence by the lack of your awareness. Opportunities can come and go. When they present themselves, think and act fast or luck will simply slip away. Time goes by and all you have left are regrets.

There are instant millionaires that most of us consider very lucky indeed. Take Lotto winners for instance. It is great luck that they struck those exact numbers. How about the lucky breed—people who inherit great fortunes handed down from their family? All of these people appear to be very lucky. But the true luck of instant millionaires starts with their ability to seek and use knowledge and advice on how to keep their fortune, and not just to keep it, but to continue to grow it so that it will support them with a comfortable lifestyle for as long as they live. Certain instant millionaires become bankrupt within a few years after winning their prize. The same happens to some of those who inherit their fortunes. This is a sad loss and is primarily due to lack of knowledge of, experience with, and responsibility in handling a large amount of money. Excessive self-indulgence of extravagant desires without proper counsel can cause trouble in paradise.

> I'm a great believer in luck, and I find the
> harder I work, the more I have of it.
> —*Thomas Jefferson*

When you are lucky please, be responsible. If you so desire to find luck, go search for it and do not expect it to just come to you. Become constantly aware of the opportunities that surround you. Luck is embedded in the action that you take to create your own future. Take a calculated risk armed with knowledge and discover your luck. Most people are too cautious to take a risk. What can make you lucky are your actions. There will always be opportunities and deals to be made. So take advantage of them and remember that your actions will assist you in finding your luck. Now is the time to give yourself a chance to start your journey in creating your own luck.

Luck does not just fall into your lap. It is something you acquire when you are searching for a better life. Use your thoughts to find luck for you, use your mind as a seat of constant positive visual images. High-quality, vivid pictures within your mind of the kind of life that you want will draw the positive forces of nature to work to your advantage in bringing those pictures to life. Thoughts are materialized into your environment. Your mental vision becomes the life that you live in. Visualize a life of happiness, abundance, and success. Make sure to use your thoughts with discipline and use your will to block negative thoughts and negative impulses. Luck happens with responsibility, discipline, and strong will power.

As I was preparing to come to America, I was ready to turn stones and find my luck. I was curious. I did not anticipate how much my life would change. Settling in Queens, New York, where a big number of Asian immigrants lived made it a bit better. I felt a sense of belonging because I seem to just blend in. Anonymity can be comforting sometimes. It did not ease my homesickness entirely though. I missed my mother dearly and I missed all the wonderful friends I left behind. Life was so fast paced that I did not have enough time to take it all in. Like a fish tossed in wild water I eventually, slowly learned to swim to where I may find a haven.

It has been a long journey to finally know that luck is something that I can create for myself. I asked myself many times, "What do I want in life? What can make me feel fortunate? What can I do to open the doors that can lead to that great path to lucky land? What are the choices that I have?" The many questions I asked myself helped me to make changes I needed in life. For some, luck may come quickly, for others it may come slowly. You have to be willing to do what it takes. In some cases, it involves risk, a change, or the willingness to do something out of the norm.

Like an inner examination, keep asking yourself questions like these:

- What can I do to make myself feel lucky?
- Do I have control of my destiny?
- What type of thoughts must I entertain to make me ready for success?
- What can I do to create more chances for myself?
- What is the difference between me and other people that seem so lucky?
- How can I change the way I think to allow me to become a more successful, happier person?
- How can I change my old limiting beliefs to make space to allow luck into my life?
- What type of people must I associate with to influence me to become successful and happy?

Answer the above questions on sheet of paper. These questions can help you examine your inner capacity to let luck become constant in your life.

> Living at risk is jumping off the cliff and building your wings on the way down.
> —*Ray Bradbury*

Find luck through:
    Awareness
    Knowledge
    Discovery
    Responsibility

# CHAPTER 38

# Positive Expectations for Life

The world you picture in your mind becomes
the world that you live in.

—*Bing Wilson*

## THE POWER OF YOUR MIND

Your mind is more powerful than you will ever know. The thoughts dwelling in your mind have a way of materializing into your life. In other words, you get what you expect. The decisions and actions that you take in each precious moment are a result of what dwells in your head, first. How you view life affects your reaction to what it is you are experiencing. Cultivate positive expectations by looking forward to each moment and each day that comes.

## MIND RULES MATTER

Images within the mind can change matter. Your mind can transform your environment. It can even transform how you look. If you want to look fit, healthy, and strong, visualize healthy images of yourself within your thoughts. The commitment that you make in living that vision depends on the intensity of your will. Keep the vision alive by using visual aids. Put an old picture of yourself in top shape some place where you can see it often, near the bed, on the dresser, or in your wallet. You can also print a picture of a body that you want and place a picture of your face on top of that beautiful body. Then in addition, recite affirmations of your desired weight each day as you look at the picture. Here is an example, "I am 120 pounds. I am healthy and fit." Repeat your affirmations three times in the morning as you get out of bed and three times at night before going to bed. You can also do extra affirmations while driving the car or while walking.

Soon you will notice becoming more aware of eating nutritious food, drinking more water throughout the day, and exercising more. You find yourself staying away from carbonated drinks and highly processed food. As your enthusiasm for health increases, you find yourself more committed to an exercise regimen. Exercising for forty-five minutes to an hour each day increases the release of endorphins from your brain. It makes you feel good and makes you highly energized. It is a natural high that gives you that extra push to do more to keep your mind and body in shape. Transform your body by using the power of your mind to give you the body that you want. Use your will and self-discipline to keep your enthusiasm and energy high until you arrive your goal.

Use your mental willpower to transform anything that you want to change. It may be your quality of life, your type of work, how much money you want to earn, or how you want to look. Use the same process to create a change and you will see the effectiveness of how the mind can rule any matter that needs to be altered.

## NOW IS ALL THAT MATTERS

Your future depends on your positive attitude and expectations that exist now. It is this present moment that counts, not yesterday nor tomorrow. Your future is embedded in each present moment. What you do now at this very moment is the catalyst to create the success and happiness that you desire. You have the potential within you to excel in what you put your heart into. The life that resides in you is complete. It is derived from perfection. A dormant seed lies in each human being waiting to be discovered. Once awareness is reached, the seed unfolds into unlimited source of knowledge, power, happiness, and abundance.

## TIME AND LIFE

I am in awe of life. It is a great gift, a gift that is so precious that I want to use my time as productively as I can for as long as I live. Time is a golden commodity that once used, is gone and cannot be taken back. Sometimes I find that there is not enough time in the day to do what I want to accomplish. This is where time management has to come in. Why do we need to manage our time? What we do now with our time accounts for what we can expect in the future. Like money put in a bank, the work that is put in now will increase the quality of how one will live in the future. What works for me is planning ahead of time. Plan each day from the night before. Try to stick to the list of what you want to do and how long you plan to do it. This process can make things get moving. You have already set your mind for the tasks and the day can go smoothly. Without planning, the many tasks that need to get done can create confusion. Get organized so you can get more things done. Life can be very good when you use your time effectively.

## CULTIVATE ENTHUSIASM FOR LIFE

Move with brisk enthusiasm as you go through your day. Great things happen to people with infectious enthusiasm and great expectations. Your tomorrows are a product of your present state of mind. Attitude is more important than the circumstances that surround you. Conduct yourself with grace even in the midst of chaos.

> A successful person is one who can lay a firm
> foundation with the bricks that others throw
> at him or her.
>
> —*David Brinkley*

Living with positive expectations increases the wonderful vibrations from within you. Your energy field sends off messages to the world around you. Opportunities are all of a sudden so visible. You start attracting great fortunes effortlessly. Welcome each moment eagerly. Open your arms to hopeful new experiences that will enhance your life.

Living with positive expectations will enhance your:
Enthusiasm
Awareness
Opportunities

I hope to have ignited the fire within you to take charge of your destiny. You now have the keys to unlock the unlimited power of your mind to create the life that you want.

Go on, get the life that you deserve. Live your life with passionate purpose to learn, love and grow. Take action. Keep on moving forward. Make the decisions necessary for you to create a positive change that can take you to where you want to be. Navigate life with love in your heart for mankind and creation. Live your life to the fullest and have great expectations. Use your energy to become an active participant in writing your new life story. Today is a new beginning. Use the knowledge, skills and techniques that you have learned from this book to materialize your ideas to propel you to greater heights. I encourage you to spread the message in this book to help open the awareness of others to the utmost possibilities of a great life. May you get the best of what life has to offer. May all your dreams come true. Good luck and God bless you.

# Bibliography

*The 7 Habits of Highly Effective People: Powerful Lessons in Personal Change*, Stephen R. Covey. 15th anniversary edition. Free Press, 2004.

*The 80/20 Principle: The Secret to Success by Achieving More With Less*, Richard Koch. Doubleday Press, reprint edition, 1999.

*Million Dollar Habits: Proven Power Practices to Double and Triple Your Income*, Brian Tracy. Entrepreneur Press, 2006.

*The Millionaire Mind*, Thomas J. Stanley. Andrews McMeel Publishing, 2001.

*Multiple Streams of Income: How to Generate a Lifetime of Unlimited Wealth*, Robert G. Allen. 2nd edition. Wiley, 2004.

*Multiple Streams of Internet Income: How Ordinary People Make Extraordinary Money Online*, Robert G. Allen. 2nd Edition. Wiley, 2006.

*A New Earth: Awakening to Your Life's Purpose*, Eckhart Tolle. Penguin, 2008.

*Real Leadership: The 101 Collection, What Every Leader Needs to Know,* John C. Maxwell. Thomas Nelson, 2006.

*Real Magic: Creating Miracles in Everyday Life,* Dr. Wayne W. Dyer. Reprint edition. HarperTorch, 1993.

*Rich Dad, Poor Dad: What the Rich Teach Their Kids About Money—That the Poor and Middle Class Do Not!* Robert Kiyosaki. Business Press, 2000. The rest of the *Rich Dad, Poor Dad* series is recommended as well.

*Secrets of the Millionaire Mind: Mastering the Inner Game of Wealth* by T. Harv Eker. Collins, 2005.

*The Seat of the Soul,* Gary Zukav. Free Press, 1990.

*Smart Couples Finish Rich: 9 Steps to Creating a Rich Future for You and Your Partner,* David Bach. Broadway, 2001.

*The Success Principles: How to Get From Where You Are to Where You Want to Be,* Jack Canfield with Janet Switzer (creators of the Chicken Soup for the Soul series). Collins, 2006.

*Top Performance: How to Develop Excellence in Yourself and Others,* Zig Ziglar, with Krish Dhanam and Bryan Flanagan. Revised and updated edition. Devell, 2004.

*Trump: The Art of the Deal,* Donald Trump and Tony Schwartz. Ballantine Books, 2004.

*Trump: How to Get Rich*, Donald Trump and Meredith Mciver. Ballantine Books, 2004.

*Unlimited Power: The New Science of Personal Achievement*, Anthony Robbins. Free Press, 1997.

*The Warren Buffet Way, Investment Strategies by the World's Greatest Investor*, Robert G. Hagstrom Jr. Wiley, 1997.

*Why We Want You to Be Rich: Two Men, One Message*, Donald Trump and Robert Kiyosaki. Rich Press, 2006.

*Your Magic Power to Be Rich*, featuring three classic works, revised and updated for the twenty-first century: *Think and Grow Rich*, *The Magic Ladder to Success*, and *The Master Key to Riches*, Napoleon Hill. Tarcher, 2007.

Now she embarks in her lifelong dream to impart her first hand knowledge to help others find the success and happiness they have been looking for. Success and Happiness Now will show the reader:

How to live life with purpose
How to forgive
How to cultivate the imagination
How to reject negative thoughts
How to have great attitude
How to conquer procrastination
The importance of learning and imparting knowledge
How to embrace change
How to materialize ideas for success

Bing Wilson believes in the unlimited resources that the universe has to offer. She wants to show the reader that anything is possible. She wants to guide the reader to prepare his or her mind to accept the new reality.

## How To Reach Us

To get more information on other Success and Happiness Now products and services that we have available, please contact us at www.successwithbing.com.

**You will find information on:**
- Books
- CDs
- How to hire Bing Wilson to speak at your next event
- How to sign up to receive weekly encouragements from Bing
- How to attend a *Success and Happiness Now* Seminar

Thank you very much for reading this book. I hope to have inspired you to use your most important resource, your mind to make the life that you desire. It is my hope to cheer you at the start as you embark on your journey. Once you get to where you want to be in your life please feel free to share your personal success and happiness story with me. With your permission I may be able to include your story on my next Success and Happiness Now book projects.

**You can also write us at:**
Success with Bing
PO Box 24
Slingerlands NY 12159

**Our phone number is:**
(518) 229-0083

## *Contribute Your Story For Our Future Book Projects*

Please feel free to share your personal story of success and happiness with us. Any story that has tremendous impact on how you live now will be greatly appreciated. With your permission, we may include your contribution to our future book projects and future electronic newsletters. Contribute your story at www.successwithbing.com.

Bing Wilson was born, raised and educated in the Philippines. She is presently living in upstate New York with her husband. Bing Wilson speaks from the heart to encourage and give hope to those who seek to find fulfillment in their lives. She teaches about the total control of the mind and its thought process as the key to creating the life that one desires. She

believes that conscious awareness of the present moment elevates the quality of life of each human being. Persuading anyone who wants to find success and happiness to live for NOW; not for the past and not for tomorrow because today is where we truly are; the only way to have a better tomorrow is to be here NOW.

She credits her mother for teaching her principles of courage, independence and perseverance as a child. Born poor, she endured hardships, living in very small quarters and sleeping on straw mats. Bing started working at the age of nine in the small deli that her family owned. Her years of hardships, has given her true lessons of conviction, faith and action.